MW00943952

Presented to:

_____

From:

_____

Date:

_____

BURN for Jesus

A 30-Day Devotional to Ignite

Fire in Your Prayer Life

By

Carla R. Cannon

CANNON**PUBLISHING**

BURN for Jesus

A 30-Day Devotional to Ignite
Fire in Your Prayer Life

By

Carla R. Cannon

CANNONPUBLISHING

DEDICATION

I dedicate this book to my daughter, Patience as a reminder that prayer is your secret weapon and key to success. No matter what, always go to God first for **Prayer + Activation = SUCCESS!**

Love, Mommy

CONTENTS

INTRODUCTION

Have you ever felt as if you needed more or struggled to maintain the little fire you currently had and couldn't seem to quite measure up to the expectations of others let alone the ones you placed upon yourself?

I too have been in a place of desiring more and wanting to go deeper in Christ and if you feel that way this devotional will be excellent for you.

Jesus longs for us to desire and pursue Him more than we do our careers (climbing the corporate ladder), relationships, friendships; etc. He is sick of our religion and boxes we tend to put Him in and He so desperately desires a relationship with us.

Take a moment and ask yourself this question: *"Is Jesus really number one in my life?"* When you open your eyes in the morning do you greet Him with praise on your lips? Or are you quick to grab your phone and check to see if you received a text message from your "boo"? Or do you dive right into your day by checking emails or social media before reverencing and thanking your Heavenly Father for allowing you to see another day?

If you answered yes to any of these questions do not feel bad for I too have been in this place and worked diligently to break these habits and replace them with habits of fervent prayer, praise and reverence. It all starts with being cognizant of our decision making as well as being intentional in our approach to drawing closer to Christ.

As you embark upon this 21-day journey, I encourage you not to skip around but to take this time seriously and allow Christ to minister to you. Deny yourself from at least one pleasurable item or activity during this time. It could be food, a person, or even your favorite television show.

Implementing fasting while completing this devotion is a great way to quiet all outside noise as you make plans to steal away on a consistent basis; just you and Jesus.

This is a great way to show the Lord that you are serious about desiring to go deeper in Him and wanting more to the point you are willing to sacrifice your time to truly *burn* for Him. Remember, if you suffer with Him, you are entitled to reign with Him. (II Timothy 2:12)

So, grab your Bible, this devotional and your Burn for Jesus Journal and get ready for the journey of a lifetime! If you have been desiring more of God position yourself to experience Him in a new way.

Be sure to read the entire chapter of whatever scripture is provided for you on the current day. For example: if Day One includes a quote from Romans 8:28, read the entire chapter 8 to gain a full understanding of what the author is saying so that this becomes a study for you as well in addition to growing deeper into God's word.

Are you ready? Let's have some fun!

WHAT IT MEANS TO BURN FOR JESUS

To *burn for Jesus* simply means to have a heart on fire for Him; a fervent passion for God and the things that involve Him. We are reminded in scripture that those who obey Him truly love Him. (John 14:21) We are living in a time that many are becoming self-indulging, puffed up and full of pride when this is so far from what the heart of our Heavenly Father truly is or what He had in mind when He created us.

II Peter 3:9 reminds us that it is not God's desire that any of us should perish but that we all should come to repentance.

As a young woman in ministry who grew up in a dysfunctional home, I know what it feels like to submit to my flesh, and cater to its needs. Therefore, after getting saved at a young age it honestly wasn't until I grew older and became more mature that I learned that despite all my failures there was nothing I could do in that very moment to cause Jesus to love me any more than what He already loved me.

If you grew up in a performance driven environment as a child, then you can relate to the

1

need or desire to base the validation of your parents upon how well of a job you did in various areas.

What I learned through reading a book entitled, Experiencing Father's Embrace by Jack Frost is the relationships we develop with our parents affect relationships we have with others as well as God; either positively or negatively.

If you are accustomed to people only loving you *when,* then you too have or are suffering from approval addiction which is my prayer that you become free from over the course of this 30-day prayer devotional.

If you are someone who has never felt good enough, pretty or handsome enough or as if you simply were not enough, you will gain authentic validation through Christ as you deny yourself food (fasting) and consecrate (set yourself apart) over the course of the next 30 days.

Unlike people, God loves us with agape - perfect, unconditional love and phileo (a Greek word that means, "demonstrated; natural affection) love.

Throughout life I have learned that often the love people tend to offer us comes with conditions-They will love us when, or they will love us if. But God's love is undying, never-ending and without stipulations and conditions.

Whether we are right or wrong, good or bad, Jesus loves us and is madly in love with us. I believe that often times as Christians we take the following scripture entirely too lightly:

"For God so loved the world that He gave His only begotten Son, that whosoever believeth in Him should not perish, but have everlasting life."
~ John 3:16

To *burn* for Jesus simply means that you identify what He did on the cross for you and even when you didn't love yourself or felt unworthy to be chosen and accepted by Him that didn't stop Him from pursuing you.

Burning for Jesus is having a passion to fulfill His mission in the earth that is identified through God's word, The Holy Bible.

Whether you are just getting the hang of what it means to develop a prayer life or if you have been praying for years, Burn for Jesus is a great devotional for men and women, young and old.

Guess what else? It doesn't stop here, Burn for Jesus (for Teens) will be available for you to share with your teenage daughters, sons, nephews, nieces; etc.

Remember, as you embark upon this new journey take it one day at a time. Do not overwhelm yourself with the cares of this world. But focus on burning for Jesus, allowing him to heal you where you hurt, provide direction or clarity as well as peace to a chaotic situation.

Keep this in mind as well: Prayer is the antidote to fear and a prerequisite for SUCCESS!

WHY A 30 DAY FAST IS RECOMMENDED WITH THIS DEVOTIONAL STUDY

Before beginning this or any other fasting regime please note this is not intended to provide medical advice or instruction. This resource is mainly to encourage you to stand on Biblical principles as it relates to the act of fasting for breakthrough. The author therefore, takes no responsibility for consequences because of actions taken by any person(s) reading this book. Please consult your physician before beginning the recommended fast.

1. What is fasting?

"And he said to them, THIS kind can come forth by nothing, but by prayer and fasting."
~ Mark 9:29

Fasting is defined by the online dictionary as the abstinence of all or some kinds of food or drink for religious observance. The Word of God gives us numerous examples of fasting and our core example, The Lord Jesus Christ, fasted for forty days and forty nights before being birthed into his ministry upon the earth in Matthew 4:2.

Fasting should be a regular part of the life of every believer not only a tradition observed at the breaking of a new year. Fasting allows individuals to deny fleshly desires and cravings and focus on feeding the Spirit instead of the body. Mankind is made up of three parts: spirit, soul and body. Whichever one we feed the most is the one that will rule our lives.

Simply put, prayer is communication with God. Prayer is often viewed as a ritual performed after waking up, before and after meals and at the *"Now I lay me down to sleep,"* point before we turn out the lights. However, prayer should be a constant communication with God, a talk that doesn't cease, as your relationship with Christ is the most valuable relationship you can ever establish.

"The fire shall ever be burning upon the altar; it shall never go out."
~ Leviticus 6:13

One way to ensure our fire never goes out is to fill ourselves with the love of God which is found through fellowship with Him which includes the study of His word, worship and fasting.

Fasting enables us to hear the voice of God clearer and receive direction/instruction concerning various areas of our lives.

Fasting also leads to spiritual breakthrough, deeper intimacy with Christ, spiritual clarity, opens our heart to spiritual revival as well as breaks Satanic strongholds.

Fasting combined with prayer and worship has many benefits which strengthen us as believers.

A scriptural guidance to fasting according to the will of God can be found in Isaiah 58:1-14, among which is highlighted the many blessings as a result of this period of fasting and sanctification. We are promised healing, righteousness, answered prayer, counsel and continual guidance, satisfaction and refreshing as a result of fasting.

As you can see fasting is a great tool for those seeking a closer relationship with God; those who desire to truly *Burn for Jesus*.

2. Identify bondage and strongholds

Bondage is anything that has power over you, things which you are enslaved to. This thing is likened to a slave master and now drives your actions and behavior. For example, unhealthy addictions like over eating, sexual immorality, lust and greed to name a few.

Sin, the hard task master that it is, will never be satisfied as its nature is insatiable. Once we taste of it, the flesh selfishly wants to always be gratified continuously driving us to crave that which can kill our body, soul and spirit.

At first, we are in control, but once you allow sin to take a test drive, it is going to override you and soon become the driver and its destination is destruction.

Strongholds and ungodly beliefs are supported by our comfort zones and can be self-inflicted prisons and at other times generational curses that need to be broken. Strongholds exist because of its resistance to the truth. T.R.U.T.H is defined as…

- Totally
- Relying
- Upon
- The
- Holy Spirit

In John 16:13 Jesus speaks of things to come and tells the disciples that when he leaves the Comforter who is the Holy Spirit will come and guide you into all truth.

Are you ready to get rid of bondage and strongholds? Burn it on the altar of surrender.

Let's face it, we all have something we have yet to fully surrender unto the Lord, so this isn't to make you feel bad but to help you identify those areas and encourage you to invite God in.

Truth is only God can help us overcome each of our struggles. I totally despise seeing others judge someone because they can't relate to their struggle. I like to say, "Your struggle may not be my struggle but as sure as you are breathing you have a struggle of some sort."

God is the master of all and can handle whatever your struggle may be. Often, we are quick to run to others for help rather than running to Christ.

Decide to run to God today and allow Him to love you through whatever you may currently be facing. You are not alone...

3. How fasting combined with prayer helps to break out of bondage & destroy strongholds

Prayer and fasting is not an obsolete approach to spiritual discipline nor is it a form of blackmail for God to grant us our desires. The main benefits of prayer and fasting are that it brings us closer to God which in turn grants us a revelation of who He is to us.

As we learn more about who God is by spending time in His word we learn who we really are.

Truth is we are all in the process of emerging into who we were created to be. The more we get to know our Creator, the more we get to know ourselves; for we are His creation.

Go to God with your fears, go to God with your dreams, vision, desires and requests. Trust Him to reveal more of Himself unto you and in turn allow it to cause you to *burn* for Jesus.

HOW TO USE THIS BOOK FOR A SMALL GROUP BIBLE STUDY

Every chapter of this book is broken down into themes including a scripture, content and guiding questions.

To customize this study for groups, use the guideline below.

Identify a group leader, outline dates, times and rules for the study group. This group is for accountability and growth together in the 30 day *Burn for Jesus* journey.

Every member should feel comfortable to share and please ensure it is clear to all members that there is a strict confidentiality clause to adhere to.

It is suggested that group size be a minimum of five (5) persons per group and a maximum of ten (10) persons. This helps keep the group intimate and easier to manage.

However, if you have a larger group, allowing attendees to share responses on a volunteer basis may be a great option to implement.

Spiritual Activation: Begin the session with an opening prayer asking for the intervention and guidance of the Holy Spirit during the Bible study.

Stirred up: Begin by using icebreakers to engage your group members with the theme. Suggested icebreakers are listed in the appendix.

Discussion: Begin the discussion by asking members how the theme and context related to them.

Burn Session: Each member highlights the thing(s) they desire to give up and in turn identify how they intend to overcome and apply the scripture in their lives.

Then, have each member write down on a piece of paper what they are believing the Lord to *burn* out of them over the course of this 30-day period and place it into a small jar. Have the leader of the group keep this and pray over it daily for 30 days (and beyond) until victory has been won in each area.

During each meeting the group will join hands and pray over everyone's entity which will offer encouragement as well as accountability in the exposed area. This is to help participants grow and develop as well as get to the root of whatever is holding them back.

No matter how small or big all participants should display the authentic love of Jesus and provide support for every party involved.

A great tip to break the ice is to open my testimonials of struggles individuals have experienced and provide strategies on how they overcame.

The key is not to isolate anyone or to make them feel bad for their current condition but to provide support, resources and agape love for them as they work through their dilemma.

Main Discussion: Each member is required on a rotational basis to study and provide additional insight into the day's theme and topic also providing additional scriptures from personal study for cross referencing and developing a greater appetite for studying The Word of God.

The presentation should be no more than seven minutes, note this is not a sermon it is simply a forum to share experiences and encourage deeper study.

Revelation is lasting and is given to obtain greater understanding and whatever is revealed through these sessions will equip you for the journey ahead.

End every session in prayer. Serve refreshments (Optional)

Virtual Options:

Option 1: This study can also be conducted virtually where the host can share live or conduct a video taking his/her audience through a 30-day devotional in the comfort of their home via social media outlets such as Facebook Live, Periscope, Instagram; etc. We recommend that you utilize free outlets to conduct these sessions.

Option 2: You can also create a virtual group on social media and share 7-minute videos of the teachings from each day with your local church, community, or supporters online. We only prefer this option if individuals do not reside in the same place.

Feel free to be creative. We don't want you to get more caught up in the method of choice rather than sharing Jesus with others through this devotional.

My final tip is to have fun getting to know God on a deeper level. If this is your first time doing a devotion commit yourself to completing the full study without skipping any days.

If you don't desire to host a group grab a friend and invite them on this 30- day journey with you as you have the fire of God ignited into every area of your life.

DAY 1
Begin All Things in Prayer

"Pray without ceasing."

~ I Thessalonians 5:17 (KJV)

To pray without ceasing simply means to never stop praying. Now this does not mean that you are to remain hidden in your prayer closet for the rest of your life and not enjoy all of God's wonderful creations.

What this simply means is to keep God on your mind all day long. Practice talking to God about everything. Luke 12:7 tells us that the very hairs on our head are all numbered.

This lets us know that God is concerned about every small detail concerning your life from who you decide to date, to what's hurting you, to what career choice you choose.

Prayer prevents us from going down the wrong path that will derail us from our purpose. Prayer is simply talking to God just like we do our friends. The struggle many people have is talking to a God they cannot see. That is where faith comes in.

Hebrews 11:1 tells us that faith is the substance of things hoped for, the evidence of things not seen. It goes on to tell us in Hebrews 11:6 that without faith it is impossible to please God, for he that cometh to God must believe that he is, and that he is a rewarder of them that diligently seek him.

In the world we live in today so many lack peace due to seeking everything but God. All that we need is found in Christ.

As humans we fail to reverence God until we are caught up in a dilemma and need Him to save us from whatever situation we have gotten ourselves in.

The Word of God tells us that God is indeed a rescue in the time of trouble (Psalm 50:15) however, we must be careful not to treat Him as a Jeanie in a Bottle and understand that He desires relationship with us.

I am a firm believer that a true relationship with Christ can keep us from getting involved in so many of the things we find ourselves in from peer pressure, poor choices and a lack of discernment.

God loves you and desires to talk with you and if you would give Him a chance and invite his Holy Spirit in to take over you will be amazed by the peace that will overtake you and dwell with you every day of your life.

I'm sure you have heard of people praying and asking God to visit them. Holy Spirit wants to dwell within us, but He can only do so when he receives an invitation.

Take time today to talk with God with confidence knowing that He hears you, he's listening, and he cares about what bothers you and wants to help you through whatever you be facing.

Give God your marriage, your struggles with being single, your health, your fear of an upcoming exam, your unruly child, issues you are dealing with on your job, a friend who recently hurt you, the death of a loved one; whatever it is lay it on the alter today.

Psalms 55:22 encourages us to cast our burden on the Lord and He shall sustain us. God is your sustainer during whatever you may be going through.

Call on Him, pray to Him, invite Him into your space. Seek Him for wisdom, guidance and direction and then journal what you hear him say.

ACTION STEPS

• What is weighing heavy on your heart today?

_____

_____

• Take a moment and write out your personal prayer to Jesus regarding this specific matter(s) that you have yet to release totally.

_____

_____

_____

_____

• Read the following scriptures and write out a new affirmation to declare over your life daily that compliments the scripture you just read.

   1. Luke 12:7

_____

_____

   2. Hebrews 11:1

_____

_____

   3. Hebrews 11:6

_____

_____

4. Psalm 50:15

_____

_____

5. Psalm 55:22

_____

_____

A Prayer for You Today

"Dear Jesus,

I praise you this morning and I thank you for your undying love for me. Even when life appears to be unfair or as if I will never make it out of my current dilemma I know I will be just fine for I am safe in your arms.

I repent for every time I doubted you. I recognize that it is a slap in your face when I second guess your instructions, doubt or become anxious of when you will make your next move.

I now understand all that I desire is found in you and there is nothing or no one that can separate me from your agape love. Thank you for your patience Jesus, and for reminding me that I belong to you and you are never slack concerning your promises.

I lift my career, business, family, financial situations, everything and everyone that is dear to me unto you now. I believe that you are the Messiah for you indeed are the anointed one.

I cast all my fears, and release all my worries and I make seeking you my number one priority. Instead of worrying I choose to war in the spirit reminding the adversary that he can't have my sanity, my family, my business, my finances or anything that belongs to me. I declare and decree this in Jesus' name. Amen."

DAY 2
Matters of the Heart

"Come to me, all you who are weary and burdened, and I will give you rest. Take my yoke upon you and learn from me, for I am gentle and humble in heart, and you will find rest for your souls."
~ Matthew 11:28-29 (KJV)

Have you ever had your heart broken in what felt beyond repair? Do you currently find yourself behaving in certain ways due to what was done to you in the past?

Life happens to all of us and it is imperative that we learn not to carry the weight of our pain with us along this journey.

Pain has a way of turning our hearts cold and shutting our spirit down from having a connection to God. Christ speaks with us through our spirit. Some call it intuition but I like to call it our "Inner Holy Ghost."

Psalms 147:3 tells us that God heals the brokenhearted and binds up their wounds. But the only way He can heal us is if we bring our heart and pain to him.

Often life happens with no explanation. Your spouse comes home and decides they no longer want to be married to you, a friend betrays you, a loved one dies, your job ends; the list could go on and on.

In your attempt to burn for Jesus you will be faced with several opportunities to shut down, blame God and even turn to religion to ease your pain.

Some turn to drugs, alcohol and even sex but once you come down off the high or the thrill is over you are still left to deal with your issue: YOU.

I like to say, it is impossible to conquer what we are unwilling to confront, and we cannot confront what we are unwilling to identify.

Just because years have gone by doesn't mean you are healed from what happened to you during your youth. There are a lot of grown men and women walking around with wounded little girls and boys living on the inside of them.

I'm sure you have heard the saying, "Time heals all wounds." I beg to differ. Wounds left unattended never heal.

Now is the time to face what has happened to you. Own it. Stop making excuses. Stop blaming yourself. Stop blaming others. Forgive yourself. Forgive them. Forgive God.

Yes, I said forgive God. Do you know how many people are mad at God because their life didn't turn out all peaches and cream like they expected?

John 14:12 says, "Verily, verily, I say unto you, He that believeth on me, the works that I do shall he do also; and greater works than these shall he do…"

Too often we have false expectations that our lives will be perfect and without tribulation. For us to fulfill the above scripture we must understand that to do greater works it will require a greater anointing.

The anointing of God is released in our lives through great trials and suffering. Just as Christ suffered we too will suffer.

II Timothy 2:12 tells us that if we suffer, we shall also reign with him…

To reign with Christ, we must be willing to suffer with him. Are you willing to go through to get to?

Whatever you are carrying today decide to release it and trust God to see you through each day of your life. Don't try to do it on your own. Holy Spirit is your helper, all you have to do is call on Him.

ACTION STEPS

• Is there anything you are currently carrying in your heart that you need to release?

_____

_____

_____

_____

• In what areas can you commit to trusting God more?

_____

_____

• Read the following scriptures and write out a new affirmation to declare over your life daily that compliments the scripture you just read.

1. Matthew 11:28-29

_____

_____

2. Psalm 147:3

_____

_____

3. John 14:12

_____

_____

4. II Timothy 2:12

_____

_____

A Prayer for You Today

"Dear Jesus,

Lord, I come to you in prayer today asking that you heal the broken places within me; the places I don't talk about much; the places I am embarrassed about; the places I've buried away.

Father, I give you permission to dig it up and heal it at the root. I repent for trying to handle matters on my end and I admit I need your help Lord. I cannot do this on my own.

Breathe life into me Holy Spirit and teach me how to allow your Word to cleanse and heal me. Make a new father. Wash me whiter than snow. I desire to be more like you.

In being like you I know I will suffer. Strengthen me to get through any trial that comes my way. I no longer try to do it on my own, but I invite you into my heart not only to heal me but also to lead me.

I trust you Lord. Thank you for your love, forgiveness, peace, power and presence in Jesus' name, Amen."

DAY 3
Maintaining Your Joy

"The joy of the Lord is my strength."

~ Nehemiah 8:10 (KJV)

In life there are so many things that come to steal our joy. I am someone who has struggled with depression much of my life, but I also remember the day when the power of God broke it off my life.

One way I maintained my deliverance was by learning my triggers and having people around me that I could be honest and confess to when I was beginning to feel down.

During this process I had to be careful not to lean more on others than I did Christ because I knew from experience that people would eventually disappoint just as I would them as well in return; for we are all humans.,

One way I learned to maintain my peace was by hiding myself in the Word of God and allowing His word to find me where I was, minister to me, wash me and mend the broken places.

I've also learned that when trouble comes it is not to destroy us but to prepare us for our next level in which Christ is calling us to. Storms never come to last, but they come with an intention to pass.

I often say happiness is based upon what happens around us and joy is contingent upon what's happening within us.

When we really burn for Jesus, we find joy in Him which in turn becomes our strength.

Be encouraged today knowing that you have so much to be thankful for. Things could always be a lot worse but by the grace of God you are still standing.

Ephesians 6:10 tells us to be strong in the Lord and in the power of his might.

Joshua 1:8 tells us to keep this Book of the Law always on your lips; mediate on it day and night, so that you may be careful to do everything written in it. Then you will be prosperous and successful.

Simply put, the Word of God is our guide and through it we find joy which in turn imparts strength into us.

Know that depression is a choice. If you have been allowing feelings of sadness to overtake your life decide today to turn things around.

Often, we are waiting on God to do what He has anointed us to do.

ACTION STEPS

• Describe a time you allowed an unpleasant situation to steal your joy.

_____

_____

_____

• Reflecting, what would you do differently the next time around?

_____

_____

_____

• Read the following scriptures and write out a new affirmation to declare over your life daily that compliments the scripture you just read.

1. Nehemiah 8:10

_____

_____

2. Ephesians 6:10

_____

_____

3. Joshua 1:8

_____

_____

A Prayer for You Today

"Dear Jesus,

Give me the strength needed to maintain my joy and to count it all joy when I find myself in various situations that to my flesh aren't very pleasant but are necessary for me to grow and mature spiritually.

Teach me how to remain steadfast and consistent in my walk with you.

Help me not to give my power away but to smile when I feel frustrated, remember to breathe and count backwards when I feel violated and to remember who I am when my identity is questioned.

Jesus, I love you and I thank you for loving me. What great joy it brings me to be accepted by you!

In Jesus' name. Amen."

DAY 4
Faith Activation

"...Be strong and courageous! Do not be afraid and do not panic before them. For the LORD your God will personally go ahead of you. He will neither fail you nor abandon you."

~ Deuteronomy 31:6 (NLT)

Declare aloud, *"I am a lot stronger than I think! I can handle a lot more than I realize! My God will never fail me therefore, failing is not a part of my DNA!"*

It is necessary that we hide ourselves in God's word daily even if for only 10-15 minutes at a time. Each of us have an adversary whom we fight daily who is constantly going before God accusing us of things we are guilty of.

But guess what? All that you and I have ever done and will do is covered under the blood of Jesus.

Recently I was thinking about just how far God had brought me from. I reflected over poor choices and mistakes I had made. Thoughts of people I had hurt and those who had hurt me began to flood my mind. In turn I began to weep and thank the Lord for during it all I was still in my right mind.

Like you, I have been through some things that if it wasn't for the grace of God I wouldn't have made it out of.

Those are the type of things that strengthen my faith. I think of how God did it for me back then and it encourages me that if He did it then he can do it again.

Psalm 37:3 tells us to trust in the Lord and do good. In all things we must choose to trust the Lord. Doubting Him is not an option.
An old hymn says, "You can't make me doubt him, I know too much about Him."

Joshua 1:9 encourages us to be strong and courageous and not to be afraid for the Lord is with us everywhere we go.

We are also reminded in Psalm 9:10 that those who know the name of the Lord and trust in Him, have never been forsaken.

Psalm 13:5 tells us of God's unfailing love and how we must put our trust in Him being reminded that He knows what is best for us.

Psalm 20:7 says that some trust in chariots and some in horses, but we trust in the name of the Lord our God.

Who do you trust on today? Is it your job? Your spouse? Have you found yourself dabbling in other religions? Be careful not to allow your curiosity to open doors of witchcraft that draw a wedge between you and the true and living God.

As you go about your day I want you to continue to whisper to yourself, "I am strong! I am courageous! I have no need to worry for God is with me! My Heavenly Father protects me!

When Satan tries to bully you, and remind you of who you are not, face him head on and remind him of who your

God is and how He's already defeated him once and will do so again!

When Satan wants to bring up your past that has already been forgiven, instead of falling into a pity party, feeling sorry for yourself simply remind him of his future for the lake of fire shall be his dwelling place! (Revelation 20:20)

ACTION STEPS

•What key areas does the adversary often intimidate you in?

_____

_____

_____

•In what ways can you increase your faith today?

_____

_____

_____

• Read the following scriptures and write out a new affirmation to declare over your life daily that compliments the scripture you just read.

1. Deuteronomy 31:6

_____

_____

2. Psalm 37:3

_____

_____

3. Joshua 1:9

_____

_____

4. Psalm 13:5

_____

_____

5. Psalm 20:7

_____

_____

6. Revelation 20:20

_____

_____

A Prayer for You Today

"Dear Satan,

I serve notice on you today. I will no longer be intimidated or threatened by you!

I realize and accept that I am the righteousness of God, I am a royal priesthood.

I am the head and not the tail, above and not beneath.

I have the power to accumulate wealth residing on the inside of me therefore, my family and I will never be broke another day of our lives!

Not only do I declare and decree this, but I activate it by refusing to believe and accept your lies anymore!

My past is now under my feet! I am forgiven because of what Jesus did on Calvary!
In Jesus' name. Amen."

DAY 5
More Powerful Than You Realize

"Behold, I give unto you power to tread on serpents and scorpions, and over all the power of the enemy: and nothing shall by any means hurt you."

~ Luke 10:19 (KJV)

I was once bound by depression off and on for years simply because I was unaware of the true power I possessed. I was not aware that the greater one resided on the inside of me and I was victorious in every battle because of what Jesus did on the cross.

Growing up in church I quoted and even memorized scripture but where I dropped the ball is I struggled with the application portion.

One day I realized I no longer had to be a slave to sin and that I could tell the devil and my flesh, *"NO!"*

You have the same ability for we both are in the fight of our lives, but you must refuse to quit and never give up!

Be reminded that God has given you the power to tread upon serpents and scorpions and over all the power of the enemy and nothing shall by any means harm you.

This means that Satan can huff and puff, but he can't blow your house down because it is established upon THE ROCK!

I feel the Holy Ghost rising on the inside of me even as I type this! This is the hour to know who you are, what you possess and who your real enemy is.

Refuse to back down, refuse to have your voice silenced and decide to stand up and fight not only for your future but for all the souls that are connected to you!

ACTION STEPS

• Identify 2-3 people you are tired of seeing Satan whip up on.

_____

_____

_____

_____

_____

• Now write out personalized prayers for each of them and declare victory over them in Jesus' name.

_____

_____

A Prayer for You Today

"Dear Jesus,

Today, I stand in the gap for _____,
_____ and _____.

I declare victory over every area of their life in Jesus' name.

I come against the spirit of fear, rejection, anger, frustration, worry, doubt, poverty, low self-esteem, insecurity; etc. in Jesus' name!

I war in the spirit on behalf of my spouse, children, pastor, friends, family, boss, co-workers, business partners; etc. and declare there is nothing missing, lacking or broken in their life!

By the power of Jesus, I declare that we have victory over the adversary!

No longer will we be blinded by his plots, plans and schemes but we ask that you expose them in Jesus' name!

Teach us how to activate all the gifts of the spirit you have placed on the inside of us Lord.

Forgive us for complaining about how hard life is when you died on a cross with thorns on your head, nails in your hands and feet and literally had your own flesh ripped from your body.

Forgive us for our selfishness. You rose again on the third day with all power in your hands and for that reason we are now powerful in you! In Jesus' name. Amen."

● Read and write out the following scriptures: John 1:12| Ephesians 1:5| Romans 15:7| Colossians 2:9-10| I Corinthians 6:17| Romans 6:6| Genesis 1:27| Jeremiah 1:5| I Corinthians 12:27| I Peter 2:9| Galatians 3:27-28| Colossians 3:1-3

DAY 6
Mindset Renewal

"That ye put off concerning the former conversation the old man, which is corrupt according to the deceitful lust; And be renewed in the spirit of your mind; And that ye put on the new man, which after God is created in righteousness and true holiness."

~Ephesians 4:22-24 (KJV)

Have you ever found yourself in a place where you felt as if you were going backward rather than propelling forward? I know what that feels like and often it is due to current circumstances and if we are not careful we will become lost in our present situation and miss what God wants to unveil to us concerning our future.

I remember feeling I was not good enough and that I did not have what it took or even that anyone would love and accept me with all my flaws. I later learned that was a lie from the enemy to keep me from living my best life.

It wasn't until I began to dig into the Word of God, search the scriptures and learn what His thoughts were concerning me that the old Carla began to slowly peel off and the new me began to emerge.

Often what we call personality is a spiritual condition in which we have become familiar with. Have you ever met someone who seemed angry or mean all the time and you concluded, Hey, that's just Sally? Or that's just the way Bob is?

What you encountered is someone whose outward expression was a direct indication of what was happening within them. You see, when we are hurting we will hurt others; but when we receive the love of God as our portion, we in turn love others.

From the foundation of the earth you were created for success, but, your environment, society and self-sabotaging tendencies have wired you for failure. These toxic thoughts show up daily or even hourly and I'm hearing you thinking out loud saying every second of the day.

I too am guilty of beating myself up through the power of my mind and through the autopilot thinking of uncontrolled thoughts. Thoughts without control result in a life without direction. Toxic thinking transcends the mind and pollutes your very environment.

Today you can decide to detox your mind through renewal by the Word and washing with the Word. There is power in the Word of God. It is much more than just words on a page; but His word is spirit and life.

ACTION STEPS

•What toxic thoughts am I allowing to pollute my mind?

_____

_____

_____

•For each toxic thought, write down a renewed thought to combat it. Challenge yourself to get an appropriate scripture to apply with this exercise.

_____

_____

_____

_____

_____

A Prayer for You Today

"Dear Jesus,

I take charge of my mind and cover it with your precious blood. I place the helmet of salvation upon my head today and every day. Where doubt has clouded my vision and perception of you and of me, I declare today I have a renewed mind. I confess that the mind in me is the same as the mind that was in Christ Jesus (Philippians 2:5). I think God inspired, God directed, and God fueled thoughts. Rejection has no place in my life and mind because I am accepted by Christ.

I guard my mind against internal and external sabotage that may be self-inflicted or inflicted by others. I uproot every negative spoken word from childhood to now and I denounce its hold over my life. I free myself of feelings of inadequacy and worthlessness and I open my heart to receive the unconditional love of my heavenly father.

Whatsoever things are honest, whatsoever things are just, pure, lovely and of good report, I think on these things (Philippians 4:8)
In Jesus' name. Amen."

● Read and write out the following scriptures:
John 6:63|Romans 12:2|Philippians 4:8|II Timothy 1:7|Jeremiah 33:3|Proverbs 4:23|Ephesians 4:22-32

DAY 7
Every Day, a Day of Purpose

"For I know the thoughts that I think toward you, saith the Lord, thoughts of peace and not of evil, to give you an expected end."

~ Jeremiah 29:11 (KJV)

Nothing you have ever been through will ever become wasted for God is going to use every experience to birth out of you what He has for you and to bring you to a place that only every experience could have helped you arrive there.

Often, we are taught that we must go back and right our wrongs when the truth is our mistakes are covered under the blood of Jesus and we are saved through His power and presence which all took place on Calvary.

When we ask God to forgive us He does just that and casts it into the sea of forgetfulness never to remember it again.

Today I want you to know that your life is worth living despite what you may be facing currently. Your life is worth every ache, pain and disappointment you may be feeling or experiencing at this very moment.

One day you will look back and saw wow! Look how far the Lord has brought me and even more how He will transform your storm into a story, your mess into a message and your pity into power!

God is a restorer and with Him by your side every day is a day of purpose!

Sure, you may have what I call character building days but even those days don't have to be all bad because you are still here, and you can use every opportunity to grow.

One thing that keeps me patient with myself is knowing that I am still growing and so are you despite your age. Refuse to become older and not grow in wisdom. Refuse to age and become set in your ways but allow Holy Spirit to reveal His will in your life for this season.

You know it or not the only person who can hinder you from reaching your purpose, is you. Each new day is not like the day before, it is an opportunity to seek and walk through a new door of purpose. It is a chance to make one step closer to the destiny plan and assignment you are designed to fulfill. For if the Lord had purposed there is no man, woman, sin and experience that can thwart this purpose except that which we give dominion.

This assurance was given when God through his might defeated the Assyrians and through the prophet Isaiah spoke this song of deliverance. What is your song of deliverance today?

A song of deliverance is a reminder that whatever you face, the good, the bad and even the ugly that "all things work together for good to them that love God. To them who are called according to His purpose." (Romans 8:28)

Begin every day with purpose on your mind acknowledging God as the author of your life. I once heard a pastoral teacher say, "the Bible is the only book where the author can be with the reader while they read it" he also continued to say that life doesn't come with "a manual" but it comes with "Emmanuel" which means God is with us (Matthew 1:23). What a relief the author of life, the creator of the universe the one who is larger than life itself assures you of his guidance.

So, sing a song of deliverance. TODAY is a day of purpose.

ACTION STEPS

• What is my song of deliverance?

_____

_____

_____

_____

• What can you do differently today to make it a day of purpose?

_____
_____
_____
_____

A Prayer for You Today

"Dear Jesus,

I submit and surrender every preconceived idea, desire and way of thinking to you. Through the power of the Holy Spirit, I make connection with your plans and your purpose for my life understanding that as the heavens are higher than the earth so are your thoughts and ways higher than mine (Is 55:8-9)

I therefore stretch my hands forth as a sign of complete surrender and I connect with the frequency of heaven to walk out your divine plan for my life.

I declare that today and every day is a day of purpose and I set my eyes upon you for guidance.

In Jesus' name. Amen."

• Read and write out the following scriptures:
Psalm 16:11|Ephesians 3:20|Ephesians
3:10|Philippians 2:13|Romans 8:28|John 10:10

DAY 8
On Earth, As It Is in Heaven

"Thy kingdom come, thy will be done in earth as it is in heaven"

~ Matthew 6:10 (KJV)

In the beginning, God created the heaven and the earth. And the earth was without form and void. (Genesis 1:1-2). It is safe to conclude that Heaven is a place of fullness, wholeness and light. All things perfect, all things beautiful and all things light. God then went on to form mankind out of the dust of the ground (Genesis 2:7) The dust of the ground can be simplified to mean earth or the particles of earth.

The Creator made mankind out of the earth, the same place where darkness, nothingness and void existed and breathed His breath into man (earth). The transformation of the earth comes when God breathes the breath a Heaven into the earthen vessels, depositing Himself into man. You are not only a carrier of God's presence on the earth, but you also can experience reflections of Heaven while on the earth. *"But we have this treasure in earthen vessels, that the excellency of the power may be of God and not of us."* (II Corinthians 4:7)

This brings a more powerful perspective to praying the Lord's Prayer which Jesus taught the disciples when they asked Him to teach them how to pray. I have for countless times prayed this prayer, read this scripture, changed and even overlooked a certain little word called "in." Somehow when I learned this prayer I always said thy will be done "on" earth. When we read scripture, every word has a supernatural revelation that brings us closer in relationship with Jesus. I now realized that when I say thy will be done in earth, I can refer to the will of God being done in me and in the place where I live (earth).

The will of God has to be first done in me and in my life to be done on the earth. The same applies to you.

It's time for the treasure on the inside of us to transcend our bodies, extend and impact our world. Because as a carrier of the fire of the Lord, we can align with His will in Heaven which was settled even from the foundation of the earth and not only pray thy kingdom come in earth but, thy kingdom come in you and me.

ACTION STEPS

•How has this scripture brought a supernatural revelation to you about the power of prayer?

_____

_____

_____

•What can you do differently to develop closer intimacy with God through prayer?

_____

_____

_____

_____

_____

A Prayer for You Today

"Dear Jesus,

I ask today, that I not only burn for you, but that you use me as a conduit and expression of your perfect love upon the earth. I activate the treasures on the inside of me which was given to manifest your power on earth.

I desire to live in the realm of manifestation that my life will reflect your grace and my words will be testament of your love. I ask you to purge, cleanse and purify me of all unrighteousness that I may be a carrier of your Holy Fire. That you would baptize me with your Holy Spirit and Fire.

Everywhere I go, I declare that your kingdom would come in me and I will be an atmosphere changer because of your presence coming alive on the inside.

I declare thy kingdom come, thy will be done in me and on the earth today.
In Jesus' name. Amen."

●Read and write out the following scriptures: Psalm 47:7-8|Exodus 15:18|I Samuel 12:12|I Chronicles 16:31|I Chronicles 28:5|Psalm 9:7-8|Pslam 45:6|Psalm 103:19|Isaiah 37:16|Daniel 4:34-35

DAY 9
An Abundance of God's Grace

"Moreover, the law entered, that the offence might abound. But where sin abounded, grace did much more abound. That as sin reigned unto death, even so might grace reign through righteousness unto eternal life by Jesus Christ our Lord."

~ Romans 5:20-21(KJV)

It is more beneficial to remedy the sin than to just reveal it. Revelations seeks to bring awareness and discovery to us yet, wouldn't it be more useful if it was alleviated and we didn't struggle in certain areas? While the law exposes our imperfection the grace of God abounds even more to sanctify from all unrighteousness.

The beauty of today's devotional is that the scripture talks of sin in the context of the past (sin abounded) since the grace of God covers what you have or are currently struggling with.

This is by no means an excuse to continue in inequity but rather encouragement to carry on in the vein of relentless pursuit of God till every impurity is burnt out by the light of His love, covered by His glory and grace would reign through us for eternity.

Your past or present by no means disqualifies you from His grace. Always remember you are in the stage of becoming, therefore, who you were, is not who you are, and who you are, is not who you will be.

Today take steps to ensure a future of eternal life through Christ Jesus and remember God's grace is sufficient for your every move.

ACTION STEPS

• Which areas in my life have been holding me back from relentless pursuit of the presence of God?

_____

_____

_____

_____

_____

•After highlighting the areas above indicate what new habit you are going to adopt to replace them. (*It is helpful to identify a scripture as it relates to this new changed behavior.*)

_____

_____

_____

_____

A Prayer for You Today

"Dear Jesus,

I   acknowledge   my   sin(s)   of
_____ before you. I admit that I am
a sinner and this problem has kept me from
realizing my true potential and living in the fullness
of your grace and love towards me. I thank you that
there is always a remedy for sin because there is no
temptation common unto man that you have not
already made a way of escape.

As I feed on your word and consecrate my heart
may I live in the freedom of your resurrection
power. That through Jesus Christ I am not only set
free, but I am free indeed. Therefore, I am free from
the guilt, shame and disappointment that sin has
placed on me.

Today, I choose to walk in the freedom of your
love.
In Jesus' name. Amen."

•Read and write out the following scriptures:
Esther 2:16-17|II Corinthians 12:8-9|Romans 3:20-
24|John 1:14|Romans 1:1-5|Acts 6:8|Ephesians
4:7|Hebrews 13:9|Ephesians 2:8-9|II Peter
1:2|Hebrews 4:16|I Peter 4:10|James 4:6|Titus 2:11

DAY 10
A Costly Sacrifice

"But the king replied to Araunah, "No, I insist on buying it, for I will not present burnt offerings to the LORD my God that have cost me nothing." So, David paid him fifty pieces of silver for the threshing floor and the oxen."

~ 2 Samuel 24:24 (NLT)

From day one through ten we have been bringing to the surface, dealing with and conquering the areas of our lives that God wants us to become victors over.

I wish there was an easier, pain free way to go through this refining process but good gold must be tried, tested and fire is all a part of the sacrifice. *"For our light affliction, which is but for a moment, worketh for us a far more exceeding and eternal weight of glory."* (II Corinthians 4:17) For years I struggled with knowing my identity and lived an affirmation thirsty life as I sought after accomplishments to satisfy my internal void.

It was at the lowest, most vulnerable and painful time of my life, that I discovered my identity. It's easy to hear an inspirational message and feel uplifted in the moment and to be ready to take on the world.

But as soon as you walk away with that message just like the sower throwing seeds that very word is waiting to be tested.

Life cannot be solely sustained from a place of inspiration but rather from a place of revelation. Revelation brings clarity on something not formally known although its effects are long lasting.

King David was responding to the plagues that were being sent to Israel by God (II Samuel 24). The prophet gave him an instruction of a sacrifice to make to the Lord to withhold the destruction.

All our substance and all we are is to the honor and glorify God. Yet a sacrifice is not a sacrifice if it doesn't cost us something then it's just a free will offering but we build an altar unto the Lord and sacrifice our heart unto Him today.

What are you willing to offer up unto the Lord today? What are you willing to release and let go? Know that often the very things we desire to hold close are the very things God desires to detach us from.

The key is not to try to do it in your own strength but to rely on Holy Spirit to be your guide and to unveil His desires unto you.

The great thing about having a heart that desires to please God is that within itself is a sacrifice because many allow their pain to dictate their actions. However, despite our pain we can choose to have a heart like our Heavenly Father by offering our lives as a sacrifice.

Be reminded today of just how valuable you are to Christ that He was willing to be beaten, bruised, spat upon just for you. It's time to take the death, burial and resurrection of Jesus personally. Declare aloud: "He died for ME!" Now receive His love on today & be willing to sacrifice or give up whatever or whoever He leads. It will all be for your benefit & unleash better into your life!

ACTION STEPS

•What are you willing to burn on the altar of sacrifice?

_____

_____

_____

_____

_____

•What does it mean to me to give a sacrifice of praise? Study Hebrews 13:15

_____

_____

_____

A Prayer for You Today

"Dear Jesus,

Today I bring a sacrifice of praise to your altar. I sincerely repent for the times I have yielded to ungodly desires and allowed them to consume and control me. I submit my life, my heart and my will to you.

Change my desire and appetite for this world and stir a hunger within me for more of you and more of your presence. Reveal unto me your desires, purpose and plan for my life and create within me a clean heart. Purge and purify my mind of all iniquity for your do not desire burnt offering but a broken spirit and contrite heart (Psalm 51:16-17) you will not despise. I humble myself

In Jesus' name. Amen."

•Read and write out the following scriptures:
John 15:13|Ephesians 5:2|Hebrews 9:28|Luke 9:24|Proverbs 21:3|I Corinthians 15:3-4|Matthew 9:13|Matthew 27:28-29|Mark 10:45|Proverbs 3:9

DAY 11
The God Who Answers

"God is our refuge and strength, an ever-present help in trouble."

~ Psalm 46:1 (NIV)

I remember growing up feeling at times as if God had forgotten all about me. Often feeling alone, I would seek comfort from various sources not knowing that God alone was enough to fill every void in my life.

We all have experienced times where it felt as if God wasn't listening when truth is when he's silent that is when He is the most attentive.

As believers it's important to remember that life is not about us but all about the purpose we were placed in the earth to fulfill. This often includes pain and suffering however, to reign with God, we must be willing to also suffer with him.

Regardless of what may be running rampant through your mind today whether it is unpaid bills, a loved one who is battling sickness, an unruly child or a pink slip you may have received from your job, know that you are the child of a *God Who Answers*.

Unlike others we are not bound by religion, but we serve a God who calls us *friend.* He is the good shepherd and we are his sheep. Learning to lay aside every weight can be a heavy task but, it is possible to achieve and master.

Being reminded that nothing you face will overtake you should bring a smile to your face and joy to your spirit. The same power that raised Jesus from the dead now resides on the inside of you. (Romans 8:11)

Therefore, I charge you to activate that power by declaring who you are in Christ! No longer are you bound by your past or current dilemma, but you are a powerful being and quitting is no option for you.

You serve a God who is there waiting on you to rely on him fully. Don't let him down. Show him that you need him. Remind him that you are helpless and powerless without him. You owe him your worship and in return He will unveil His glory.

ACTION STEPS

• What is heavy on your heart today?

_____

_____

_____

_____

_____

• What is it that you need God to do for you today?

_____
_____
_____
_____
_____
_____

• What are you willing to offer Him in return?

_____
_____
_____
_____
_____

A Prayer for You Today:

"Dear Jesus,

Today I come to you laying all my fears, doubts, concerns and worries at your feet. I give you my whole heart. I tug at your heart asking for an abundance of your love.

Teach me to love like you, trust like you, respond like you, live like you. I acknowledge that my life is not my own and it is to you that I belong, and I want to burn for you Jesus.
Reignite my fire, my passion and help me go deeper in you. When life throws rocks at me teach

me how to catch one and stand on it in faith knowing I will not be overtaken by the enemy for you are my rock and it is in you that I place all my trust.

In Jesus' name. Amen."

•Read and write out the following scriptures:
Psalm 46:1| II Timothy 2:12|I John 5:14-15|Psalm 66:19|John 9:31| I Peter 3:12

DAY 12
The Squeeze of God Releases the Hand of God

"For I reckon that the suffering of this present time is not worthy to be compared with the glory which shall be revealed within us."
-Romans 8:18 (KJV)

Do you currently find yourself in a place where you feel, or it seems as if you are in a tight squeeze? You can't move forward, you won't dare go backward and literally all you seem to be able to do is move your head from side to side.

Have you ever felt that you had more bad days than good days and in turn you felt as if it was some type of punishment toward you?

If you answered yes, know that you do not stand alone in this thought process that has plagued many. Today I'd like you to reconsider how you view trouble (your problems.)

We are reminded in scripture that the suffering of this present time is not worthy to be compared with the glory that shall be revealed within us.

What does this mean? It means that all you are currently facing is nothing compared to the blessings God has for you.

The enemy sends trouble in the form of distractions however, God sends trouble to strengthen, mature and shape us into who we were created to be.

It's not the happy times in life that we grow but it's during our toughest moments that growth occurs.

Unlike the adversary, the squeeze of God does not come to destroy you but to prepare and employ you to your destiny. Understand that being squeezed by God is not a comfortable or even an enjoyable place. It may literally feel as if your very soul is being gutted out.

Relax...embrace it. The squeeze of God releases the hand of God. That my friend is how you end the battle with a mighty victory! Stop all the kicking and bucking and surrender.

Give God your whole heart. Yes, even the portion you try to keep to yourself for when you want to do things your way. He my friend is the way; the truth and the light so remember trials don't come to break you, but they come to make you more like Him. Suffering is a great way to be set on fire for Jesus. For out of your pain births purpose, patience, greater sense of determination and love. The squeeze of God removes all forms of self-sufficiency and teaches you to rely totally on God for *everything.*

ACTION STEPS

• What storm are you currently facing?

_____

_____

_____

_____

• What scriptures can you apply to your direct situation(s)?

_____

_____

_____

_____

_____

_____

A Prayer for You Today

"Dear Jesus,

I admit feeling your squeeze is not always comfortable, but I trust you with my life. I no longer desire to be full of selfish motives, but I want to be strengthened and develop mental toughness so no matter what I can follow your footsteps ensuring I represent you well.

Sure, sometimes I feel as if your squeeze is going to kill me. But suddenly I'm reminded of just *how much you love me and that you'll never tempt but you test me to ensure I am being a good student over all that you are teaching me.*

Forgive me for the times I complained or reacted as if being chosen by you was a curse. I now understand I am blessed beyond measure and I'd rather experience your squeeze to become transformed into your image than to stay the way I am and miss my opportunity to burn for you.

In Jesus' name. Amen."

●Read and write out the following scriptures:
Romans 8:18|James 1:1-2|II Timothy 2:12|Romans 5:3-4|Psalm 34:19|I Peter 5:10|II Corinthians 4:17|I Peter 4:1|I Peter 3:14|Philippians 1:29|Matther 10:38

DAY 13
Just Enough Light for the Step I'm On

*"I will instruct you and teach you in the way you
should go; I will guide you with My eye."*

~ Psalm 32:8 (NKJV)

Too often we desire to know the completion of a
thing before we are willing to step out and do it.
Over many years of walking with God I've learned
that His nature is to establish trust within us.

Within His word He tells us that without faith it
is impossible to please Him. This means that we
must learn to trust God to see us through all He
directs us to do without having all the details up
front.

Another thing I've learned is often it's not that
we don't want to obey God, we simply don't want
to disappoint Him.

During the process of learning to discern the
voice of God there will be times you will miss it
and that is perfectly okay. God understands that you
and I are in a process of becoming what He has
already predestined we would be.

This is where grace is applied. The grace of God
releases the hand of God. Never allow fear to

cripple you or keep you from doing what you feel deeply in your heart to do.

Sure, there will be feelings of uncertainty but use it as fuel and to focus like more than ever on what you feel Holy Spirit is leading you to do or not do.

Now more than ever is the time to embrace fear and use it as momentum to soar. Never allow fear to keep you back from living the abundant life Christ has died for you to live. Don't worry about having all the answers you just focus on walking and allow God to do the guiding and trust Him to give you just enough light for the step you are on.

ACTION STEPS

•What BIG thing do you feel led to do today (this year?)

_____
_____
_____
_____
_____
_____

• What one thing can you do that will change everything?

_____
_____
_____

A Prayer for You Today:

"Dear Jesus,

I admit that I often overanalyze a situation rather than simply obeying your command. So many times, I have tried to figure things out instead of trusting your word to lead and guide me to my ordained place.

Today I choose to release all anxiety and fear and vow to obey your word as you give me just enough light for the step I'm on. Show me your way father. Give me peace as a sign that I am on the right path. It's not so much that I am afraid of failing; I am afraid of failing you.

Wrap your arms around me Jesus and grant me the courage to move forward knowing that all I need is found in you.

In Jesus' name. Amen."

●Read and write out the following scriptures:
Psalm 32:8|Joshua 1:9|II Samuel 7:28|Psalm 9:10|Psalm 20:7|Psalm 31:14|Proverbs 3:5-6

DAY 14

Choosing to Love Again

"Jesus Christ is the same yesterday and today and forever."

~ Hebrews 13:8 (KJV)

In life we will disappoint others and we too will be disappointed. Like you, I have experienced hurt that pierced my soul in which I initially felt was beyond repair.

Have you ever been cut so deep by someone that it left you questioning God and if your relationship with Him was as solid as you thought?

Unfortunately, many people blame God when others disappoint them when he is clear in His word that in this life we will experience many troubles. He then encourages us to be of good cheer and put our trust in Him because He has overcome the world.

Perhaps you have experienced betrayal in a friendship or even your marriage. Or maybe you weren't protected as a child and the very one that was supposed to protect and cover you abused and neglected you.

I know what each of those things feel like and there is only one way to overcome it all. By choosing to forgive and love again.

Sure, it's easier said than done when it comes to forgiving others when they cut us deep. One way that I have found the strength to do this is because of how much I've needed God to forgive me. I have been lost, totally did my own thing and needed God to forgive me, cleanse and purge me as well as settle my spirit when I was literally all over the place.

Often, we as humans tend to treat God the way others have treated us when the reality is He will never fail us. God of this universe is incapable of making a mistake.

Despite your heart ache or fear to love again you can take a step today to release those who hurt you and allow the love of Jesus to fill you.

Talk to Jesus just like you would a friend and share with Him your heart. Be bold and courageous today by choosing to love enough. There is nothing scarier than to look in the eyes of your abuser and yet still choose love rather than hatred. This is what it really means to burn for Jesus.

ACTION STEPS

• Who do you need to forgive today?

_____

_____

_____

_____

• What offenses have you carried in your heart that you know you need to let go of today?

_____

_____

_____

_____

A Prayer for You Today

"Dear Jesus,

Forgive me for not choosing to love others the way you have loved me. I admit my heart has been broken to the point I thought honestly that it was beyond repair.

There were times I dared to love again because the pain was so severe but then I met you and the love you extended to me I couldn't help but share it with others.

Teach me to choose love in all things. To never retaliate against my enemy, or go tit for tat with a naysayer but to turn a deaf ear to every accuser and choose forgiveness and love instead of bitterness and hatred.

In Jesus' name. Amen."

●Read and write out the following scriptures: Hebrews 13:8|John 3:16|Psalm 86:15|Deuteronomy 7:9|Psalm 136:26|Zephaniah 3:17|John 15:9-17|Romans 5:2-5|Romans 8:37-39|Galatians 2:20| I John 3:1|I John 4:7-8|I John 4:9-11|Romans 5:8

DAY 15
Enemy Exposed

"So that Satan will not outsmart us. For we are familiar with his evil schemes."

-II Corinthians 2:11(NLT)

One benefit of prayer is learning the heartbeat of God as well as have him speak to us. The Word of God is the voice of God however, many seek the voice of God without ever opening His word and learning what He has to say regarding various subject matters.

The Word of God tells us that God will not have us ignorant of Satan's devices therefore, we must pray for supernatural discernment so that we may know what is really going on around us.

Scripture goes on to tell us that we must know no man after the flesh but by the spirit. I have found this to be true. In our flesh we are all flawed however, the spirit of a person is the true essence of this existence.

Sure, there is then the mind, will and emotions that often override the spirit depending on whichever one is being fed the most.

One of the many things I love about prayer is hearing God speak to me through His word, a prophetic worship song or even an inspirational book.

God will use anything to gain our attention but it's up to us to have an ear to hear to receive direction or even instruction.

There's absolutely no way you and I can spend time in the presence of God and He not reveal His plan to us. He will even take it a step further than that and reveal the plan of the enemy if we will have an ear to ear.

In the book of Revelation, we see repeatedly, the words, He that has an ear let him hear what the spirit of the Lord is saying to the church.

We are the church and we must learn to seek God on our own to the point it becomes so natural just like breathing. We don't think to breathe, it is simply something we do subconsciously. In the same token, spending time in prayer and seeking the face of God through reading His word and worship must become second nature where we do it without even thinking.

Our relationship with God is our lifeline but it is up to us to see it as such. God desires for us to get to know Him beyond a Sunday worship experience. He desires to walk with us in our everyday lives.

Therefore, we must refuse the bait of Satan as well as reject his lies to think that we don't serve a God who loves us and cares about every area of our life.

The Bible tell us that every hair on our head is numbered. That to me is confirmation that he is concerned about my life beyond a worship service.

God doesn't want us to just experience Him once a week but daily, but we must accept truth that He is available to us no matter how imperfect we may feel.

Choose to see the enemy for who he is today which is as a wolf in sheep's clothing. No need to waste energy trying to find him for eventually it will get hot and he will come running out of there if you maintain your stance in the spirit rather than focusing on defeating him in your flesh.

ACTION STEPS

•In what areas is the enemy fighting you today?

_____
_____
_____
_____
_____

• What can you do to build yourself up in these areas?

_____

_____

_____

A Prayer for You Today

"Dear Jesus,

Father, I thank you for exposing my enemy. Thank you for showing me that everyone who smiles in my face is not my friend and does not have my best interest at heart.

Teach me how to see and not always share, to hear and not always repeat but to armor up in prayer, fasting, being a studier of your Word and an ambassador for your cause.

I thank you Lord that you will not have me ignorant of Satan's devices, but you have exposed him, and I praise you that my eyes are open. No longer will I connect with others who mean me harm out of the desperation of being accepted.

But father I thank you for your love, joy, peace and favor that surrounds me, and everyone connected to me.

In Jesus' name. Amen."

●Read and write out the following scriptures:
II Corinthians 2:11|John 10:10|Revelation 2:7|James 4:7|I John 4:4|II Corinthians10:3-5|I Peter 5:8-9|Isaiah 54:17|Ephesians 6:11-17|Romans 8:37|I Corinthians 15:57|II Thessalonians 3:3|Luke 10:19|Matthew 18:18

DAY 16
God's Art, His Masterpiece, You!

"O house of Israel, cannot I do with you as this potter, saith the Lord. Behold as the clay is in the potter's hand, so are ye in mine hand, O house of Israel."

~ Jeremiah 18:6 (KJV)

When the artist begins the first stroke of the masterpiece those looking on have no idea what's on his mind. You see, in his eyes, he has already seen this finished piece before its actual conclusion. Those observing the creative process may even be puzzled as to why he paints each stroke, fashions the handle and curves each piece over and over until its reality matches his vision at conception.

This is our reality as God's masterpieces. Having no clue what the finished "you" is but trusting the potter who has the skill to fashion every imperfection into the finished product. He smashes the pottery from time to time because the value of this art is in the working of his hand.

Trusting a God, you can't see can be tough at first; however, once we commit to studying His word and learn that He is not apart from His word and began to study his character and seek His

79

presence and purpose for our lives we become more at ease.

The great thing about God is He never allows any experiences to go wasted; He uses them all. Romans 8:28 tells us that all things work together for the good of those who love the Lord and are called according to His purpose.

We must understand that in the midst of all we may be facing, God is there, and He is using situations, trials and even our setbacks to develop us into His precious masterpiece.

Today you may feel the pulling, pushing, tugging or even smashing in your life. Instead of giving the credit to an illusionist (Satan) submit to God as he is making you into exactly what He created you to be.

Know that your life has substance and you were created for a purpose and to see it fulfilled in your life a commitment to studying God's word and spending time in His presence is what invites Him to expose more of Himself to you.

Many often say they don't *feel* God but understand this faith is not a feeling but a knowing. We must have faith that all of God's word is true and there is comfort in knowing you were created by God, for God into His beautiful masterpiece.

Your life has purpose, meaning and you have an assignment in the earth that only Holy Spirit can reveal. Too often many focus on their gifts which comes without repentance (Romans 11:29) but the true essence of who we are is in the spirit as well as the depth of our soul (mind, will and emotions.)

Know today that you are unique, handmade by God and He can handle whatever you are facing today. During it all, embrace the plan of God for your life knowing you are indeed his great masterpiece and He will use all your pain for His Glory Story!

ACTION STEPS

• What are the areas the potter is molding in my life?

_____
_____
_____
_____
_____
_____

• In what areas of my life can I be more submissive to God's creative process?

_____
_____
_____
_____

A Prayer for You Today

"Dear Jesus,

Today as I feel pushed, pressed and smashed, I realize that you are doing a complete work in my life and that which you do is well done. I commit my life into the hands of the potter and I make the necessary adjustments today as guided by your Holy Spirit to come into alignment with your vision for my life.

I denounce the work of my flesh as it no longer has the power to fashion me outside of your design. I put every fleshly desire under subjection. Today, I come into agreement with what is on heavens mind concerning me and I declare that the things that come into my life today is in complete alignment with your plan and your will.

Even in adversity, I will keep praise on my lips knowing that all things work together for my good. I snatch back my dominion and walk in the power, authority and redemptive work of the cross of Jesus Christ.

In Jesus' name. Amen."

●Read and write out the following scriptures:
Jeremiah 18:6|Romans 8:28|Romans 11:29

DAY 17
Building *God* Habits for Successful Living

"The Lord is good unto them that wait for him, to the soul that seeketh him."

~ Lamentations 3:25 (KJV)

Why worry? Why get flustered and stressed? The God of the universe is at your side. As a matter of fact, he dwells within you. Instead of thinking of how much further you could have been, what mistakes or wrong decisions you made, guess what you are on a comeback. Your purpose for life and the place of ultimate fulfillment is in Him.

In life it is so easy to fall into a pity party and begin to rehearse the should of, could of, would of; but instead focus on learning the lesson from every trial.

It has always been my prayer to master turning my wounds into wisdom and to use it to become better instead of bitter.

Everything in life boils down to our daily habits. What we do on a consistent basis unveils who we are at the core. I'm sure you have heard that we are what we repeatedly do. I disagree with this from the aspect of the spirit vs flesh; supernatural vs natural.

Who we are in the flesh is our sinful nature however, as we spend more time in the presence of the Lord, we exchange our nature for His nature and become more in tune with the things of the spirit which unveil the depths of our soul.

Often, we experience salvation but never really submit to having our souls purged and healed which is our mind, will and emotions.

When we come to Christ true our spirit is now renewed and we are forgiven of all our sins however, to maintain that freedom we must allow God the opportunity to continue the great work He started in us (Philippians 1:6) He shall finish it however, it takes a lifetime to do so.

Our mind becomes renewed through the reading/studying of God's word, which in turn washes our soul and strengthens our spirit. We are encouraged to live according to the spirit and not the flesh (Galatians 5:25) and the only way to do this is to develop God habits that will lead to successful living.

Next, we have our will; once surrendered to Christ on the day we receive salvation we must continue to surrender our will to Christ by exchanging ours for His.

This may sound easy, but life happens and there will be times you will want to do things your own way but a principle of daily submission unto Christ in prayer, fasting, worship, healthy fellowship with other believers will strengthen your core and lead to great decision making.

Lastly, there is our emotions for a long time I was trying to shout out, cry out and stomp out my innermost pains that I later learned with emotional heartbreak due to my childhood.

When it comes to emotional healing it takes time to heal however, too many Christians tend to focus on their spirit and neglect the needs of the soul. The true essence of who you and I are is found in the depth of your soul (mind, will and emotions.)

Could it be that you are in the need of deep soul healing and cleansing? I have been there and what this simply means is partner with God to work through your issues rather than suppress them and pretend that everything is okay.

This could include talking with a therapist, a mentor in the form of a coach who specializes in assisting others in doing their *soul* work. This topic is often taboo in the Christian community and I believe this is why so many live defeated lives.

But you don't have to. It is possible to develop God habits and live a successful life. God habits are simply exchanging your way of doing things for God's way of doing things and sure it will get tough but the more you deny your flesh the stronger your spirit becomes.

It is possible to love what God loves and hate what he hates but that only comes with spending time in His word and learning His true character and how to echo his voice and heartbeat in the earth.

The great thing about God is it doesn't matter how we start but all that matters is how we persevere and refuse to give up first and foremost on ourselves.

The beautiful thing about God is He knows you inside and out and yet…still, He chooses YOU! Isn't that something to be glad about? You don't have to perform or do anything to win God's love. He offers it to you freely.

It is perfectly okay to desire to be successful in life but understand success without God leads to temporary satisfaction. Your relationship with Christ is what will sustain you in your marriage, single life, in your career, relationships, raising your children and more. Therefore, seek Him first in all that you do, and success will be inevitable for you! (Matthew 6:33)

3 Ways to Build *God* Habits in Your Life:

1. Study God's word
2. Apply God's word
3. Walk out God's word
4. Repeat Steps 1-3 daily

ACTION STEPS

- What areas of my life have I compartmentalized and left God out of?

_____
_____
_____
_____
_____

- What God habits for success are you going to implement today?

_____
_____
_____
_____
_____

A Prayer for You Today

"Dear Jesus,

I admit that I need you. I desire to know you on a deeper level; in a more intimate way. I don't want to simply attend worship services and my life never change.

I want to encounter you, learn your ways and echo your voice in the earth. Teach me how to love like you, forgive like you, be fearless like you.

Activate the strength, wisdom, courage and love within me that has been there all along.

I repent for trying to do things on my own for I am nothing without you Jesus. I need you in my life. I want to know you intimately, as Abba; Father.

Give me a thirst for righteousness sake. I exchange my way of doing things for your way. Lead and guide me Lord and I will follow you. Sharpen my discernment of your spirit and voice in my life.

Please forgive me for the times I have tried to make things happen on my own in my own strength. I admit I am burnt out by trying to be self-sufficient. I come to you in total surrender receiving your strength which is perfect in my weakness.

I break down the walls and compartments, I have built up and I let you in to every area of my life. I trust you with all my heart and I ask you to guide my steps this day.

Help me to recognize that every good idea is not a God idea. Quicken me in my discernment to make decisions guided by you.

In Jesus' name. Amen."

• Read and write out the following scriptures: Lamentations 3:25|Philippians 1:6|Galatians 5:25|Matthew 6:33

DAY 18
Free Yourself

"If the Son therefore shall make you free, ye shall be free indeed."

~ John 8:36 (KJV)

Too often in life we walk around carrying false burdens; things that God never intended for us to carry. Sure, we have all messed up but once we repent we are forgiven.

Today, I encourage you to forgive yourself for anything you have ever done. Forgive yourself for the things you have never verbalized or whispered "I'm sorry."

The great thing about God is He does not hold our past against us. The Word of God tells us there is therefore no condemnation to them which are in Christ Jesus, who walk not after the flesh, but after the Spirit.

Condemnation is defined as the expression of very strong disapproval. God never comes to condemn but He does come to convict and correct. Although there are times that you and I may disappoint or disobey God His love toward us never changes. God hates the sin not the sinner.

Conviction on the other hand is what we feel when we know we have not done what is right. You may have heard this referred to as intuition, but I like to call it our *Inner Holy Ghost.*

Holy Spirit is our guide in the earth and He will always let us know when something is off or not right. Have you ever met someone and thought to yourself, I don't know what it is about them; I can't put my finger on it, but something is off?

Most of the time when the spirit of suspicion is not in play it is our Inner Holy Ghost alarming us to be careful and if we will remain prayerful in time (if not right away) God will reveal it to us.

The problem is we don't remain in God's presence long enough to get an answer or to experience true freedom and deliverance.

Today I encourage you to free yourself from all past and present mistakes. God is not only a God of a second chance but His mercy for us endures forever.

He loves you immensely and there is nothing you can ever do to turn off His love for you. Often, we compare how people treat us to how God would treat us. Truth is people do not always properly represent God and if we will be honest, you and I don't always do so great of a job either.

The great thing about a relationship with Christ is we experience new mercies every day.

There are so many people who walk around with guilt and shame when God has already forgiven them. I invite you today to free yourself of this burden and receive the love Christ has for you.

You don't have to beg God; only ask. His word tells us so in Matthew 7:7-8 to ask and it shall be given, seek and we shall find, knock and the door will be opened.

I encourage you to ask God for what you need today and expect Him to grant it unto you. Know that He may not always show up in the way you expect Him to but with a discerning spirit you'll always recognize Him when He does. Learn to see God in all things and life will have a much brighter perspective and grant even greater opportunities for you.

Next, I encourage you to seek the face of the Lord and find strength, power and joy in His Word. The Bible tells us in the beginning was the Word, and the Word was with God, and the Word was God. That means that in seeking the face of God you are searching scriptures to learn the heartbeat of God.

God desires to unveil Himself to you. All He needs is an invitation. He no longer has to be your mother, father or grandparents' God. He desires to be your personal Savior.

What Christ did on Calvary we must begin to take personal and ponder the fact that He literally laid down His life for YOU. No one took it, but He offered it as a sacrifice to free us from our sins. What a mighty God we serve!

Lastly, I invite you to knock on the door of God's heart and express your love for Him. You'll never have to worry about rejection because He has loved and accepted you before the foundation of this earth. Even in your mother's womb He knew you.

Nothing you have ever done can separate you from the love of God. Once you repent, you are covered by the blood of Jesus.

Today is a new day of grace, mercy, favor and opportunity. You serve a God who looks beyond our humanity and covers us with His divinity. No matter where you have been or what you have done receive His love and forgiveness today and walk into the newness of all He has for you!

ACTION STEPS

• What self-inflicted condemnation do you need to let go of today?

_____

_____

_____

_____

•Identify exactly what you are forgiving yourself for today. Write it below.

_____

_____

_____

_____

_____

A Prayer for You Today

"Dear Jesus,

Today I ask you to forgive me for (insert below exactly what you desire forgiveness for) _____, _____, _____, _____,

_____,_____,

_____, _____, _____, _____ and _____. *I release my sins before you father. I no longer try to hide them. I acknowledge your presence in my life Lord.*

It is you who has kept me over the years. Without you where would I be.

I ask that you help me forgive myself for the things I've mentioned above as well as things that I have failed to mention. Bring all things back to my remembrance Father so that I may lay them at your feet.

My desire is to please you. I want to be free God. I desire more of you and less of what this world has to offer. Teach me how to be a true CHRISTian Lord. To emphasis you in all that I do. Not only in word but more so in deed.

Teach me how to treat others right even when they fail to do so to me. Teach me your ways Father that I may never depart from them.

I freely receive your love for me today as you cover me with your banner of love. Jehovah Nissi I call you in this office today as you cause me to have an experience with your unconditional love towards me.

Heavenly father I ask for the gift of faith to become activate in my life that I may walk in the confidence and freedom of who you have called me to be and not allow my past or present reality to hinder me from the fullness of your promises towards me.

I repent of the times I have condemned myself and allowed negative thoughts to cloud my ability to see your beauty. I have the mind of Christ therefor I think God thoughts and my life reflects your grace, your love and your peace.

In Jesus' name. Amen."

● Read and write out the following scriptures: John 3:17|Romans 8:1|Lamentations 3:22-23|Matthew 7:7-8|Jeremiah 29:11|Romans 8:31|Proverbs 3:5-6|John 1:1

DAY 19
Let Them Go!

"Forbearing one another, and forgiving one another, if any man has a quarrel against any: even as Christ forgave you, so also do ye."

~ Colossians 3:13 (KJV)

The hardest thing I've ever had to do in my life was to extend forgiveness to individuals who did not seem remorseful for what they had done to me.

Can you imagine what it was like for King David when he learned his son Amnon had raped his half-sister Tamar who was the sister of his son, Absalom; who later murdered Amnon out of retaliation.

That's tough right? This one family endured the tragedy of not only a rape but also a murder and guess what? David never really dealt with it which could have been what led his son Absalom to take matters into His own hands.

What do you do when you were violated by someone who should have protected you and no one comes to your defense?

What helped me forgive my father for abandoning me? What helped me forgive my mother for choices she made during my childhood that I didn't feel best suited my older sibling and me? What helped me forgive people I befriended only to be used for my platform or women whom I trusted only to later find out they shared my secrets with others. What do you do when forgiveness is hard to do?

What helped me that I believe will also help you is reflecting over my own life. I did not always treat people right. Sure, I had been betrayed but I had always been a betrayer. Sure, I had been lied on, but I also lied on others. Sure, I had been taken advantage of but there were also times I had taken advantage of others.

It wasn't until I learned how badly I needed God's forgiveness that I learned I could not afford to hold on to the offense of others not if I truly wanted to be forgiven.

Although we don't talk about it often bitterness and unforgiveness is what leads to infirmities and physical ailments in our body. We hold people hostage in our soul rather than releasing them unto the Lord.

How do we hold them hostage? By replaying what happened repeatedly in our mind, by choosing to be bitter rather than better because of what happened, to allow our hearts to turn cold because of what someone else did or didn't do.

Oftentimes when life happens we make excuses as to why we made certain mistakes we made. Truth is, we do things because we want to do them whether it is to relieve the pain, extend payback to those who hurt us; which hurts us more in the end.

Know this, anyone you refuse to release from your heart and soul have power over you. It may sound hard but who said you had to do it alone? Ask God today to help you extend grace, forgiveness and mercy to those who have wronged you.

Please note that forgiveness does not mean reconciliation. You can forgive and move on with your life.

The only person you are in control of is yourself so make sure you always have control since this little matter can open the doors to bitterness, rejection and shame which then makes you a prime target for evil spirits and manifested seeds of this potent yet poisonous harvest.

Let them go. You may be harboring resentment against someone who has since released you. Turn this burden over to Christ today and trust Him to heal your broken heart.

ACTION STEPS

• Take a deep breath in and out and for each person you need to release list the names below.

_____

_____

_____

• Identify below exactly what you are forgiving them for.

_____

_____

_____

_____

_____

_____

A Prayer for You Today

"Dear Jesus,
I release _____, _____,
_____ and _____ in prayer today.
As I have received your forgiveness Lord help me to forgive those who have wronged me.

I free myself of the bondage of bitterness and un-forgiveness today, I am full of love and compassion and you love flows to me and through me to those I encounter.

I also forgive myself for things I have done, said or thought against others in the past or even my present. Father help me to become more like you.

Teach me how to forgive and resolve matters more quickly rather than allowing them to linger over a course of time which ends up becoming a burden to me.

Father, I cast all my cares upon you Lord and declare that I have come to the complete end of myself. I desire to know you in a greater way. I desire to be filled with your anointing, power and presence that will enable me to live a victorious life today and every day.

I declare that I am healed, whole and delivered.

In Jesus' name. Amen."

● Read and write out the following scriptures:
Colossians 3:13|Matthew 6:14-15|Luke 17:3-4|Ephesians 4:31-32|I John 1:9|Isaiah 43:25-26

DAY 20
Steadfast and Unmovable

"But none of these things move me, neither count I my life dear unto myself so that I might finish my course with joy, and the ministry, which I have received of the Lord Jesus, to testify the gospel of the grace of God."

~ Acts 20:24 (KJV)

In this race of life many hurdles and obstacles will come our way to test and through the process strengthen our faith in God. Yet overcoming each of these though at times difficult, teaches us reliance on God. This journey would have encouraged you to develop unmovable, impenetrable and stable positions in God's love towards you though which you can make a difference not only in your life but in the lives of those you may meet.

A house built on a solid foundation though subject to violent storms will still stand. There is always hope for the hopeless, rest for the weary and strength for the weak in God's presence. Even though it looks dismal and gray, there is a silver lining. In these things, be steadfast and unmovable pressing toward the mark through Jesus Christ.

ACTION STEPS

• What life storms are you facing?

_____

_____

_____

_____

_____

•Write a short prayer below releasing your current burdens unto the Lord.

_____

_____

_____

_____

_____

_____

A Prayer for You Today:

"Dear Jesus,

I am steadfast and unmovable through your spoken and written word to me. In all things I consider myself an overcomer and conqueror. Despite what it may look like today I see through heavens eyes that it is already better.

I release wholeness over myself, my family and friends today and declare completion of your *assignment for me on the earth. I release discouragement and stand secure knowing that no height, no depth, no principality of power can separate me from your love.*

I curse untimely death and abortion of purpose. I confess that I am secure, I am steadfast, and I am unmovable.

In Jesus' name. Amen."

• Read and write out the following scriptures: Hebrews 10:23|I Corinthians 15:58|II Timothy 2:15|I Corinthians 4:2|Hebrews 3:14|I Thessalonians 3:5

DAY 21
Awakening the Warrior Within

"And it shall come to pass afterward, that I will pour out my spirit upon all flesh; and your sons and your daughters shall prophesy, your old men shall dream dreams, your young men shall see visions."

~ Joel 2: 28 (KJV)

Are you ready to truly experience the revival in which Christ is ready to release in your spirit? It is time for all of us to step out of our comfort zone and no longer seek the validation of others.

Did you know your blessings are found on the other side of your comfort zone? What God has placed within you is too great to be minimized. Now is not the time for you to shrink back but to spring forward operating in your full potential of what Christ has assigned for you to do in the earth.

What Christ has placed on the inside of you is about to be awakened! Isn't that exciting? You have prayed for this moment and it is here my friend. It doesn't matter who said you couldn't, for God said you can!!!!!

I can remember believing the lies of the enemy that God couldn't use me because I was a teenage mother. I later learned that was a lie and it was actually because of the things I had done that God could use me. Not only that He was going to use it all for His glory. Guess what else? He is going to do the same for you!

True growth is not determined during seasons when everything is going well. But it is determined when our world is flipped upside down.

Therefore, we must never despise our valley experiences because it is those moments that unlock, unleash and activate the warrior within us.

Every trial you have experienced was never to kill you but rather to help expose weak areas and show you where to apply more of the Word of God in your life so that you can be equipped and ready for battle!

I shared on social media today that "Your pain didn't come to hinder you but to help you!"

Embrace every challenge, struggle and set back and use it as ammunition to be propelled forward. All that you are currently facing is simply to awaken every gift, talent, ability and anointing that has been there all along.

WARRIOR COME FORTH!

ACTION STEPS

• What is it that you would like the Lord to awaken within you?

_____

_____

_____

_____

_____

• What are you willing to lay down at the feet of Jesus today?

_____

_____

_____

_____

_____

A Prayer for You Today

"Dear Jesus,

Today I ask you Jesus to set a fire deep down in my soul that I literally cannot contain or control. I want to completely lose myself in you Jesus.

I desire to know you in a deeper way. No longer do I want to fall apart when storms begin to rage in my life or become down when naysayers plan my *demise. But teach me how to allow the storms of life to awaken the warrior (fighter) within me.*

I admit sometimes I can be timid but I long to be strong, mighty and fearless like David, focused and obedient like Nehemiah, plentiful and prosperous like David and persevere against all odds like Job.

Lord, I ask you today to Awaken the Warrior within me! I am tired of the same ole' same ole.' I need a change. Renew the right spirit within me. Make me over Jesus until I look just like you.
Jesus, I want to burn…for…you…

In Jesus' name. Amen."

● Read and write out the following scriptures:
Psalm 46:1-3|Proverbs 18:10|Nehemiah 8:10|Ephesians 6:10-12|Psalm 23:4|Isaiah 43:2

DAY 22
Purpose Activation

"The thief's purpose is to steal and kill and destroy. My purpose is to give them a rich and satisfying life."

~ John 10:10 (KJV)

Often, we read the above scripture and stop after the word destroy. Truth is God's desire is for us to live a rich and satisfying life when can be found only through a relationship with Him.

The word rich don't always mean money. You can be rich in love, joy, peace and even the presence of the Lord.

Today I want to challenge you to change your perspective as it relates to your purpose and life. We were created to glorify the Lord and one way He enables us to do this is by placing gifts and talents within each of us.

My question to you is what are you doing with what God has given you? One way to activate your divine gifts is to (1) Recognize them and (2) Begin to use them.

The more you use your gift the more comfortable you'll become in using it. One way we sharpen our gifts is to use them.

I invite you to use the gift of love, forgiveness, peace, patience and even longsuffering as you go about your daily life along with your natural gifts.

Include God in everything you do and take Him everywhere you go reminding yourself that every day is a life of purpose!

Now, that you've been activated, go and activate someone else! Let them know they can begin to live and no longer exist!

Remind them that Jesus loves them and that the pain they are currently experiencing is only to activate purpose within them!

Let them know they are not alone for God is with them and will never leave nor forsake them.

ACTION STEPS

• What do you feel your purpose is in the earth?

_____

_____

_____

_____

• What are 3 ways you could use your gifts to help others?

_____

_____

_____

A Prayer for You Today

"Dear Jesus,

Thank you for activating me deeper into purpose. It is my desire to walk out your desire in my daily life. I want what you want. I want to please you in how I conduct myself both privately and personally; at home or at the market (and beyond.)

Lord, I pray that you will use my life to touch the lives of many. Now that you have activated purpose within me, show me how to activate it in others!

Teach me your ways Lord so that I can in turn teach others. Let my light shine bright today to draw others to me so I can in turn draw them to you. Take my life Jesus, and use it for your glory.

In Jesus' name, Amen."

● Read and write out the following scriptures:
John 10:10|Psalm 16:11|Jeremiah 29:11| Ephesians 2:10| Philippians 2:13| Romans 8:28

DAY 23
The Hurt That Healed Me

"But God hath chosen the foolish things of the world to confound the wise; and God hath chosen the weak things of the world to confound the things which are mighty."

~ I Corinthians 1:27 (KJV)

Have you ever found yourself in a place where you didn't understand what God was doing nor why He allowed certain things to transpire?

If you answered yes, I too have been there along with thousands of others on the planet. We never understand how God is going to use our pain, disappointments or even our setbacks and turn them around for our good.

Throughout my short time on this earth one thing I have learned is that no experience is a wasted experience.

Everything you and I have faced (including what you may be facing right now) God is going to get the glory out of it.

I know it may not seem like it, look like it or even feel like it but it's true.

Every hurt that you've felt has the potential to bring you closer to Christ and in doing so leads you to a place of healing.

There have been countless times I've found myself in a low place only to learn that God used it to shift me from the direction I was going and redirect me where He wanted me to go.

Know today that whatever you are facing, it's there to heal you.

Whether it's an unfavorable diagnosis, a spat with your spouse, an unruly child; whatever it is…ask God "Lord, what is it that you are trying to teach me?"

Trust me, He will answer you and show you how not only does your pain have purpose but also how the very thing the adversary designed to suck the life out of you, you have the power (through Holy Spirit) to transform it into life itself!

You are an overcomer and there is nothing too hard for God to accomplish in your life. Because He resides within you there is nothing impossible for you!

ACTION STEPS

• What pain are you currently experiencing right now?

_____
_____
_____
_____
_____

• In what ways have you identified that your pain has purpose?

_____
_____
_____
_____
_____

A Prayer for You Today

"Dear Jesus,

Thank you for your undying love for me. Reveal to me how my pain has purpose and how you desire to get the glory out of my life.

I desire to please you in all that I do. I love you Jesus. Make your way known unto me Lord.

Show me how to use all I have gone through to help others come through what they may be going through.

In Jesus' name, Amen.

● Read and write out the following scriptures:
I Corinthians 1:27| Romans 8:18| Jeremiah 29:11| Psalm 34:18| Psalm 147:3| Revelation 21:4|Psalm 23

DAY 24
The Power of FOCUS

"I will lift up mine eyes unto the hills, from whence cometh my help. My help cometh come from the Lord, which made Heaven and earth."

~ Psalm 121:1-2 (KJV)

Now is the time in which you and I have to fight for focus like never before. With screams from reality TV and social media we struggle to give undivided attention to our loved ones as well as current tasks at hand.

The next time you feel distracted I encourage you to pause, take a deep breath and refocus by telling yourself, *this* is what matters the most to me.

Whether it is time set aside for personal growth and development, fitness training or beyond choose to be present 100% in every task you set out to do.

ACTION STEPS

• In what ways have you currently lost focus?

_____

_____

_____

_____

_____

- Identify 3 ways you can refocus and realign with the will and purpose of God for your life.

_____

_____

_____

_____

_____

A Prayer for You Today

"Dear Jesus,

I admit sometimes I lose focus and tend to give my problems more of my attention than I do you. I am aware that whatsoever I magnify becomes big in my world.

Today I choose to magnify you Lord. I choose your ways, your word and your will for my life.

Teach me how to focus on the good rather than all the bad that is in the earth.

Teach me how to shift my perspective now and give my full attention to all you have called me to do.

Father I thank you for loving me despite the many times I get off track.

Help me to extend the same love, level of grace and patience to others just as you have extended to me. `

In Jesus' name, Amen.

• Read and write out the following scriptures: Psalm 121| Colossians 3:2| Matthew 6:33|Proverbs 4:25|Psalm 1:1-6|Romans 8:5|II Timothy 2:15| Philippians 4:8|Matthew 6:24|Proverbs 2:2-5

DAY 25
Overcoming Digital Traps

"For all that is in the world, the lust of the flesh and the lust of the eyes, and the pride of life, is not of the Father, but is of the world."

~ I John 2:16 (KJV)

So often we tend to get caught up in all that is happening around us. We begin to compare our current living conditions to someone else's living condition. We compare our spouse to someone else's spouse. We compare our children to someone else's children and so forth.

It is important not to get caught up in believing all the hype that we see on social media. Online is the one place where people can pretend to be whoever and whatever they desire to be.

Realistically, who is going to post all the bad that is going on in their lives? Who is going to post a pic with tears streaming down their face saying, "Today, I'm downtrodden, I feel forgotten and I'm extremely depressed."

Instead a photo of them and "bae" will be posted as if they are living the life when in reality "bae" didn't even come home last night.

This is one way the enemy sets what I call "digital traps" in our mind because he attacks us psychologically.

You ever scroll on social media having an absolutely great day, then come across the profile of a celebrity who uses foul language, has been known for cheating on their spouse and yet by the time you go through every one of their photos you end up hating your entire life?

I know this may sound comical, but it is sad and true because this is how powerful social media has become. Many have been caught up in the façade of "I have to portray that I am living this dream life."

Truth is, no matter how much money someone has in the bank or how famous they become, life happens to every single one of us.

Money doesn't keep cancer from knocking at your door, your prominent status doesn't always keep your spouse from delivering divorce papers at your door.

So, my friend, be mindful today as you "scroll" and know that although some may be appearing to live the dream life, you have Jesus and experience His peace daily is the ultimate life that many are seeking.

Money runs out… people die, relationships and friendships end… but the love of God will endure forever!

ACTION STEPS

• Whose profile do you tend to compare your life to? (Come on, be honest, we all have done it. The only way to overcome it is to first acknowledge it.)

_____

_____

_____

_____

_____

• Identify 10 things you love about your life! (It's not as bad as it may seem once you really think about it.)

_____

_____

_____

_____

_____

A Prayer for You Today

"Dear Jesus,

Thank you for allowing this book to shift my perspective and cause me to redirect my focus on what really matters.

I admit there have been times I have compared my life to others and coveted what they have. This isn't something I am proud of however, I now understand that I can not conquer what I am unwilling to confront, and I cannot confront what I am unwilling to identify.

Strengthen me in every area in which I am weak and teach me how to be thankful for all that you are and all you are doing in my life.

I rebuke the spirit of comparison from my life and I release a spirit of thankfulness and gratitude in Jesus' name.

Lord, I am blessed beyond measure and it is all because I have you. You are bigger than the car I drive, the home I live in, the clothes that are on my back.

You are bigger than anyone's opinion of me and for that I am extremely thankful!

Thank you for all you are doing in my life Lord. I am who I am by the grace of God. It's not about my name being on the billboards for you are the true and only shining star.

In Jesus' name, Amen.

● Read and write out the following scriptures:
I John 2:16|John 10:10|Ephesians 5:11-12|John 7:24| Matthew 18:15-17|John 4:1|Matthew 7:21-23

DAY 26
Ignite My Fire Lord

"You shall love the Lord your God with all your heart, with all your soul, and with all your mind."

~ Matthew 22:37 (KJV)

Do you currently feel as if you are in a place where your passion is diminishing, and your world seems to be crashing down?

If you haven't, then keep living and you will. Life has a way of bringing us closer to Jesus. I like to view my tests and trials as a way for God to get my attention to either teach me something new or give me an opportunity to walk out what He has taught me in His word.

No matter what is on your heart today know that it was never designed to pull you away from the Lord. It was just the opposite; to draw you closer to Him.

Whatever you feel that you have lost, I encourage you to lay it at the feet of Jesus today. Maybe you are going through a tough time or feel as if you don't know if you are going or coming.

Life has a way of putting a tight squeeze on us, but I dare you to turn that pressure into praise! Trust

God to get you through the process! Declare aloud, "Ignite my fire Lord! I want to burn for you!"

That's what it's all about; burning for Jesus. To have a heart on fire for Him. To want what He wants, reject what He rejects, love what He loves and hate what He hates.

Use your current situation as an opportunity to get to know God in a way that you've never known Him before. Allow your trials to bring you closer to Him; not cause you to drift away down your own path.

ACTION STEPS

• In what ways do you need to be ignited?

_____

_____

_____

_____

_____

• How can you change your perspective regarding what you are facing right now?

_____

_____

_____

_____

A Prayer for You Today

"Dear Lord,

I desire to be more like you. I ask that you cleanse me of every impurity and anything that would keep me from your presence.

I admit sometimes I don't always do what I should, but I also recognize that I need your help.
I repent for trying to be holy in my own strength instead of coming to you for help.

Thank you for loving me when I didn't love myself. Thank you for keeping me when I didn't want to be kept.

Father, I thank you for all things and it is in Jesus' name I pray, amen."

Read and write out the following scriptures:
Joel 2:28|Matthew 5:44|John 3:16|John 14:15|John 15:9|Romans 5:8|Romans 13:10|I Corinthians 13

DAY 27
Forgiveness is for You, Not Them

"And let the peace of God rule in your hearts, to the which also ye are called in one body; and be ye thankful."

~ Colossians 3:15 (KJV)

I can't tell you how many countless days I wasted being angry with people who I felt had wronged me only to find out they were out enjoying their life while I was at home crying over what they had done to me.

To free yourself, you must extend forgiveness. I know you may be saying, "But you don't know what they did to me!"

Think about all we have done to Christ and, yet He still forgives us. Not only does He extend His love, but also grace and forgiveness.

There will be some things in life that will be hard to get over it but don't try to do it alone. God's word brings healing, clarity and understanding.

I can't promise you that it all will make sense. But what I can promise you is that the Word of God works when we work the Word.

Only the Word of God could soften my heart to forgive my father for being inconsistent in my life. Only the Word of God could cause me to forgive my stepfather who physically abused me during my childhood.

Only the Word of God could cause me to continue to love on people after experiencing intimate betrayal from people I once called friends.

Life is all about how we respond to it. Trust me, whatever you are dealing with there is someone, somewhere dealing with something ten times worse.

It really could be worse but by the grace of God whatever you are facing it is because you were built to handle it.

One reason you must forgive is to free yourself. Forgiveness is for you, not them. Whether you ever receive the apology or not, you can take your concerns to the Lord in prayer, release that person (or people) and trust God to heal your heart.

It's when we choose to hold on to our hurt and pain that the enemy gains a foothold in our lives.

Choose forgiveness today!

ACTION STEPS

• Who do you need to forgive today?

_____

_____

_____

_____

_____

• Write a letter of forgiveness below
(If it's extended, continue in your Burn for Jesus Journal)

_____

_____

_____

_____

_____

A Prayer for You Today

"Dear Jesus,

I thank you for this day in which you have made. I will rejoice and be glad in it.

Lord, I lay down every mean and hurtful thing that has ever been said or done to me.
Although I may never forget some of the things that were done to me, I ask that you'd help me forgive.

I don't want to be angry Lord. I don't want to walk in unforgiveness. Teach me how to extend the level of grace to others that you extend to me.

I give you all glory, honor and praise. In Jesus' name. Amen."

Read and write out the following scriptures:
Colossians 3:15|Matthew 6:14-15|Luke 17:3-4
|Ephesians 4:31-32|I John 1:9| Isaiah 43:25-26 |Acts 3:19|Isaiah 1:18|II Corinthians 5:17

DAY 28
Speak Life!

"Death and life are in the power of the tongue; and they that love it shall eat the fruit thereof."

~ Proverbs 18:21 (KJV)

Jesus formed the world by the words He spoke. Therefore, that lets us know words are containers of power.

We have the power to speak life or death in our life as well as the life of others.

What if I told you whatever you are facing currently, you could change your perspective (mindset) and change the words you speak which could lead to a change in your situation?

Even if your situation doesn't change, you can allow it to make you stronger in the process.

One way I remain encouraged is by practicing speaking the opposite of what I speak. I could be feeling down right depressed, but I will declare aloud, "This is the day the Lord has made! I will rejoice and be glad in it!"

I know you may be like, really? Trust me, it works! Combining inspirational declarations with the Word of God can literally shift the trajectory of your life.

It is impossible to be pitiful and powerful at the same time. Therefore, I encourage you to speak life into all you meet whether boy or girl, man or woman, rich or poor and beyond.

Being kind will attract kindness to you. In all things SPEAK LIFE!

ACTION STEPS

• What kind of thoughts do you currently have about yourself?

_____

_____

_____

_____

_____

_____

• Replace any negative thoughts with positive ones and practice declaring them aloud for the next 7 days.

_____

_____

_____

_____

_____

_____

A Prayer for You Today

"Dear Jesus,

Lord, I pray that you would guide my tongue today and help me to only speak words that edify your people. Let me not be puffed up with pride or filled with anger or anxiety.

I lay aside every weight today Father. Although, life happens to all your children, I understand it is our attitude that determines how we get through difficult seasons.

I am determined to count it all joy and lean and depend on you and not my understanding in Jesus' name.

Father, I thank you for an anointing to live according to your word and I thank you for releasing understanding and revelation knowledge according to your word.

Father, I cancel every word curse that has ever been spoken over my life and those that I may have spoken over the lives of others.

Please forgive me Lord and remind me everyday of my life that words are containers of power.

In Jesus' name, Amen."

Read and write out the following scriptures:
Proverbs 18:21|I Peter 3:10|Colossians 4:6|
Ephesians 4:29|Proverbs 10:19|Proverbs 15:4|
Proverbs 15:28|Proverbs 17:9|Matthew 15:11|

DAY 29
Breaking the Cycle

"Brethren, I count not myself to have apprehended: but this one thing I do, forgetting those things which are behind, and reaching forth unto those things which are before."

~ Philippians 3:13 (KJV)

Have you ever found yourself in place where you kept going around and around the same mountain to no avail?

Perhaps you have witnessed others continue to pursue a path that has proven not to work for them.

In life we all find ourselves in cycles at one point or another.

Cycles can occur within our mindset, attitudes, habits, relationships, friendships, behaviors and beyond.

The key to breaking habits is to learn a better/new way of doing things. Being someone who is committed to personal growth, I have learned that to overcome in an area I must first recognize that a problem exists.

For you to break whatever reoccurring cycle that is in your life you must be honest and admit there is need for change.

You can never conquer what you are unwilling to confront, and you cannot confront what you are unwilling to identify.

ACTION STEPS

• What cycles need to be broken in your life?

_____

_____

_____

_____

_____

_____

• How can you change your perspective regarding what you are facing right now?

_____

_____

_____

_____

_____

_____

A Prayer for You Today

"Dear Jesus,

Thank you Lord for loving me enough to reveal the real me to me. Often, I can be so caught up in what I want others to believe about me that I fail to acknowledge the truth about myself.

I thank you for loving me despite the real me. You never judge me or even disown me even when some of the things I do bring you ultimate embarrassment.

Help me father to commit to change, to desire what you desire and want what you want.
Show me how to overcome so I can in turn help others who may be bound.

I thank you for your true and living Word Lord and I decide to stand on it every day of my life, in Jesus' name, Amen."

Read and write out the following scriptures:
Philippians 3:13-14|Isaiah 43:18-19|II Corinthians 5:17-18|Luke 9:62|Psalm 37:1-6| Romans 8:1| Romans 8:28| Proverbs 3:5-6| Psalm 32:8

DAY 30
Everyday a Day of Worship

"I will lift up mine eyes unto the hills, from whence cometh my help. My help cometh from the Lord, which made heaven and earth."

~ Psalm 121:2 (KJV)

Did you know that everything we do can be a form of worship? From how we treat ourselves, to how we treat others, to what we do and so on.

Worship is anything we do for the glory of God. Too often worship is viewed as something you do during a Sunday morning church service.

However, worship is so much more than that. Anything that would put a smile on God's face is a form of worship.

I encourage you today to take notice of everything you do today: As you are driving down the road, dealing with your co-workers, planning out activities with your spouse and engaging with your family; view every activity as an act of worship.

Doing so will bring you great joy especially knowing that you were created to worship the Lord. Never allow the enemy to make you feel that your life doesn't matter because that is the furthest from the truth.

You and I were created by God, for God and it is through Him in which we move and have our being.

Be reminded of God's love today. Know that He loves you beyond measure and He desire the very best for you.

Know today that everyday can be a day of worship. Worship the Lord with your mind, worship the Lord in your deed, Worship the Lord with your mouth. Worship the Lord with your obedience.

Embrace the warmth of God's smile knowing that He is pleased with you and desires to know you more intimately.

ACTION STEPS

• How can you express love and appreciation to God today?

_____

_____

_____

_____

•In what ways can you increase your worship unto the Lord?

_____

_____

_____

_____

A Prayer for You Today

"Dear Jesus,

I acknowledge your presence Lord and I am honored to be called your child.

Thank you for your patience all the days of my life. Teach me how to take advantage of precious moments I have with you.

Shift my perspective, make me over, increase my sensitivity to your voice.

Show me how to worship you in my expression of love toward others.

Open my heart to your word Lord. I desire more of you. I ask that you fill my cup until it overflows.

I desire to look like you, sound like you, act like you, extend grace to others like you; and so much more!

I admit I don't always get it right; sometimes I get it wrong. But, you still love me.

Father, I thank you now in Jesus' name, amen."

Read and write out the following scriptures:
I John 2:16|John 10:10|Ephesians 5:11-12|John 7:24| Matthew 18:15-17|John 4:1|Matthew 7:21-23

SPIRITUAL WARFARE BOOKS RECOMMENDED

The Holy Bible
(Life Application Bibles are a plus)

The Rules of Engagement by Dr. Cindy Trimm

Prayers That Rout Demons by John Eckhart

Spiritual Warfare by Richard Ing

Unshakeable by John Eckhardt

Everyone's Guide to Demons & Spiritual Warfare
by Ron Phillips

Deliverance and Spiritual Warfare
by John Eckhardt

Fasting by Jentezen Franklin

How to Fast Successfully by Derek Prince

Commanding Your Morning by Dr. Cindy Trimm

The Bait of Satan by John Bevere

Battlefield of the Mind by Joyce Meyer

Fervent by Priscilla Shirer

APPENDIX
Icebreaker Exercises

Use the flame template illustrated below and cut out flames to be distributed to each group member. Feel free to be creative with your flames. This is a symbolic icebreaker exercise for the things we are going to burn on the altar of sacrifice for the next 21 days.

Distribute a flame to each team member and have them write what it is they will be burning in turn for a closer relationship with God. After they have written the things down on the flame deposit it in a bag, basket or tin and shake it up. The leader will then read out the areas not to embarrass anyone in the group as the exercise is anonymously done. Always remember to establish that it is a safe place for accountability, transparency and growth.

If you choose, you can do a symbolic act of burning the flames (please exercise all necessary fire precautions and use caution if you intend to do this suggested act). This symbolizes the commitment that at the end of the 21 days the Fire of the Holy Spirit will consume all these areas. (Optional)

BIBLICAL REFERENCES TO FIRE

This trivia type challenge will help identify and highlight place in the scripture where fire references were made. Team members are stretched to identify the symbolism of fire in each reference.

Moses and the burning bush – Exodus 3:2
Elijah calling down fire on Mt Carmel – 1 Kings 18
Three Hebrew boys fiery experience – Daniel 3
Day of Pentecost Fire – Acts 2

Discuss other example of fire in the Bible and its meaning.

JOIN THE MOVEMENT

Join the *Burn for Jesus* movement simply by sharing the love of God everywhere you go.

This world needs a Savior and one way we can present Christ to them is through love. Many are hurting, discouraged and lacking peace but as a believer we carry the spirit of Christ within and can impart it into others through kind gestures, friendly conversations, intercession and more.

If you were blessed by this devotional, consider hosting a small group bible study with your women's group or some of your friends to grow closer to Christ.

Also, if you are active on social media consider hosting a live study with your audience and invite others to grab their copy at www.CarlaCannon.com.

For special group pricing pleased email: Carla@womenofstandard.org or call 888-502-2228.

ACKNOWLEDGEMENTS

I am truly thankful to God for allowing me to journey throughout life with much grace and never allowing the storm to overtake me. Abba, I am grateful for your undying love for me and I thank you for counting me in when others counted me out!

To my mother, Evangelist Felicia C. Hagans, thank you for never leaving my side and always believing in me even when I didn't believe in myself.

To my Bonus Dad and Pastor, Richard Hagans, I believe Heaven is smiling upon us because hell lost after launching major attacks. I am excited about what is to come for us!

To my one and only sister, whom I absolutely adore, Latisha Coward, I am proud to be your little sister. Growing up I had you to protect me and even fight a few of my battles for me but now I have learned to stand on my own and I hope that makes you proud. I will always be your baby sister.

To my daughter, Patience Harris. You are an amazing gift to me and I thank you for always loving me and never losing respect for me as your mother even after witnessing my lowest moments.

To my Spiritual Father and Mentor, Bishop R.C. Blakes, your love, support and shared wisdom has healed the little girl within. Because of your guidance, prayers and unconditional love my family has been restored and I have become a better woman, daughter, friend and mother. Thank you for loving me and always reminding me that what was in me was greater than any obstacle presented before me.

To everyone who has ever supported anything I have done; thank you. To my Women of Standard Ambassadors, I thank you for rocking with me and standing with me during various transitions in my life. Thank you for respecting me as your leader and praying for me and extending encouragement during my most painful moments.

To everyone who doubted me, thank you. Because of you, today I have much stronger prayer life and know God in a way I wouldn't have never known Him before. Pain has a way of birthing purpose and because of you I have birthed out not my dream but God's assignment for my life!

MEET THE AUTHOR

Carla R. Cannon, "The Trailblazer" is known as Your Marketplace Mentor and is indeed one of *God's Moguls* in the making. She is the visionary of the *Burn for Jesus* movement. With her eloquent yet transparent approach she is committed to empowering global women from the pulpit to the marketplace on how to operate authentically and un-apologetically in their divine calling from the pulpit to the marketplace with a spirit of excellence.

Carla is the mother of a beautiful teenage daughter, Patience whom she loves dearly and spends most of her time with whom she calls "Queen Pay."

Carla R. Cannon Enterprises, LLC is her brand in which she houses Cannon Coaching & Consulting (where she coaches women on how to bankroll their brilliance and bulletproof their business as a Kingdom Entrepreneur), Cannon Publishing (where she teaches aspiring authors how to write a best-selling book in 7 days as well as how to transform their book into a lucrative business), and Women of Standard (a global movement where Carla's mission is to get women unlocked, unleashed and activated into purpose from the pulpit to the marketplace!

The testimony of this young woman of faith and her ability to share her story unashamed and with such boldness and conviction is truly what causes her to connect with others on multiple levels.

Whether she is speaking to an audience of 1 or 1,000 the energy Carla exudes is magnetic, and contagious for she always leaves her audience not only feeling hopeful but with the tools to pursue their dreams and move further into their path of purpose.

Carla is truly a woman after God's own heart and lives her life not trying to correct all her wrongs but to learn and grow from them daily to reach others to help them overcome!

Carla has been featured on multiple radio and talk shows including The Jewel Tankard Show (featuring Jewel Tankard from BRAVO's hit show, Thicker Than Water.) Carla has also shared the stage with many prominent leaders such as Dr. Yvonne Capehart, Real Talk Kim, Jekalyn Carr, Tera C. Hodges, Dr. Jamal Bryant and more in which the Lord is raising her up for such a time as this!

147

In 2014 Carla was invited to cover media for Bishop T. D. Jakes' annual Woman Thou Art Loosed Conference where tens of thousands of women and men assembled together. Carla's message is simple: No matter what you are in, you can come out and recover ALL!

Learn more about Carla at
www.CarlaCannon.com!

Stay Connected:

Follow her on Periscope by downloading the app and searching: Carla R Cannon

Twitter, Facebook, Instagram, Periscope:
@CarlaRCannon

You Tube Channel: Carla Cannon

Made in the USA
Columbia, SC
15 February 2020